POET IN NEW YORK

POET IN NEW YORK
(*Poeta en Nueva York*)

Federico García Lorca

Translated by
Pablo Medina and Mark Statman

Grove Press
New York

A Note on the Text
The Spanish text included here (on which this translation is based) is the one that
appears in *Obras Completas,* Federico García Lorca, Tomo I, edited with notes by
Arturo Del Hoyo (Madrid: Aguilar, 1986).

Versions of some of these translations appeared in: *Tin House, Subtropics, The Florida
Review, Teachers & Writers,* and *The American Poetry Review* (APR).

Printed in the United States of America
Printed simultaneously in Canada

FIRST EDITION

ISBN-10: 0-8021-4353-9
ISBN-13: 978-0-8021-4353-2

Grove Press
an imprint of Grove Atlantic
154 West 14th Street
New York, NY 10011

groveatlantic.com

A la Nena   (P.M.)

For Katherine and Jesse (M.S.)

Contents

Foreword by Edward Hirsch   xi

Introduction   xv

I. POEMAS DE LA SOLEDAD EN COLUMBIA UNIVERSITY   2
I. POEMS OF SOLITUDE AT COLUMBIA UNIVERSITY   3
   Vuelta de paseo   4
   Back from a Walk   5
   1910 (Intermedio)   6
   1910 (Interlude)   7
   Fábula y rueda de los tres amigos   6
   Fable and Round of the Three Friends   9
   Tu infancia en Menton   14
   Your Infancy in Menton   15

II. LOS NEGROS   18
II. THE BLACKS   19
   Norma y paraíso de los negros   20
   Norm and Paradise of the Blacks   21
   El rey de Harlem   24
   The King of Harlem   25
   Iglesia abandonada (Balada de la Gran Guerra)   34
   Abandoned Church (Ballad of the Great War)   35

III. CALLES Y SUEÑOS   38
III. STREETS AND DREAMS   39
   Danza de la muerte   40
   Dance of Death   41
   Paisaje de la multitud que vomita (Anochecer de Coney Island)   48
   Landscape of the Vomiting Crowd (Twilight at Coney Island)   49
   Paisaje de la multitud que orina (Nocturno de Battery Place)   52
   Landscape of the Urinating Crowd (Nocturne of Battery Place)   53
   Asesinato (Dos voces de madrugada en Riverside Drive)   56
   Murder (Two Voices at Dawn on Riverside Drive)   57
   Navidad en el Hudson   58
   Christmas on the Hudson   59
   Ciudad sin sueño (Nocturno del Brooklyn Bridge)   62

City Without Sleep (Nocturne of the Brooklyn Bridge)   63
Panorama ciego de Nueva York   66
Blind Panorama of New York   67
Nacimiento de Cristo   70
Birth of Christ   71
La aurora   72
Dawn   73

IV. POEMAS DEL LAGO EDEN MILLS   74

IV. POEMS OF LAKE EDEN MILLS   75
Poema doble del lago Eden   76
Double Poem of Lake Eden   77
Cielo vivo   80
Living Sky   81

V. EN LA CABAÑA DEL FARMER (Campo de Newburg)   84

V. IN THE FARMER'S CABIN (Newburgh Countryside)   85
El niño Stanton   86
The Boy Stanton   87
Vaca   92
Cow   93
Niña ahogada en el pozo (Granada y Newburg)   94
Girl Drowned in the Well (Granada and Newburgh)   95

VI. INTRODUCCIÓN A LA MUERTE
Poemas de la soledad en Vermont   98

VI. INTRODUCTION TO DEATH
Poems of Solitude in Vermont   99
Muerte   100
Death   101
Nocturno del hueco   102
Nocturne of the Hole   103
Paisaje con dos tumbas y un perro asirio   108
Landscape with Two Tombs and an Assyrian Dog   109
Ruina   110
Ruin   111
Luna y panorama de los insectos (Poema de amor)   114
Moon and Panorama of the Insects (Love Poem)   115

VII. VUELTA A LA CIUDAD   120

VII. RETURN TO THE CITY   121
   New York (Oficina y Denuncia)   122
   New York (Office and Denunciation)   123
   Cementerio judío   128
   Jewish Cemetery   129
   Pequeño poema infinito   132
   Small Infinite Poem   133
   Crucifixión   136
   Crucifixion   137

VIII. DOS ODAS   140

VIII. TWO ODES   141
   Grito hacia Roma (desde la torre del Chrysler Building)   142
   Cry Toward Rome
   (From the Tower of the Chrysler Building)   143
   Oda a Walt Whitman   148
   Ode to Walt Whitman   149

IX. HUIDA DE NUEVA YORK
   Dos valses hacia la civilización   158

IX. FLIGHT FROM NEW YORK
   Two Waltzes Toward Civilization   159
     Pequeño vals vienés   160
     Small Viennese Waltz   161
     Vals en las ramas   164
     Waltz in the Branches   165

X. EL POETA LLEGA A LA HABANA   168

X. THE POET ARRIVES IN HAVANA   169
   Son de negros en Cuba   170
   Son of Blacks in Cuba   171

Acknowledgments   175

Notes on the Poems   177

Futher Reading   183

Foreword

Federico García Lorca spent a critical nine months in New York (June 1929–March 1930), and created from the experience an indelible work of art, an agonized spiritual tribute to the urban milieu, a ferocious testament. Lorca was extremely energized and deeply appalled by the city he discovered—its "extrahuman architecture and furious rhythm," its "geometry and anguish"—and the work he left behind still carries a sense of shock and surprise, a weird feeling of recognition, after all this time.

Pablo Medina and Mark Statman have given us a marvelous new version of Lorca's anguished masterpiece, *Poet in New York*. The destruction of the twin towers of the World Trade Center, the wake of September 11, 2001, sent them back to the great poetry of New York City, especially Lorca's fiery symphonic cycle, which was mostly created in the midst of the Great Depression. Lorca spoke of "a poet in New York," but he recognized that he might just as well have said "New York in a poet." So, too, we might say that New York has lived inside these translators, two poets who have recast his work in the light of a traumatized American city. Lorca had at different times considered calling his book *The City* (*La Ciudad*) and *Introduction to Death* (*Introducción a la muerte*) and, indeed, death and the city are its twin inspiring presences, which is one of the reasons that Medina and Statman find it so disturbingly relevant. Their translation is a major reclamation. They have given us a *Poet in New York* for our time.

Lorca always recalled his stay in New York as "one of the most useful experiences" of his life. It was his first trip abroad. He called New York "Senegal with machines" and said that all of his native Granada could fit into three skyscrapers. He felt "murdered by the sky." He was stunned by the vastness and scale of the city, which was for him a place where during the day people were mired in mindless games, fruitless labors, and at dusk poured into the streets in a human flood. Lorca's tenderness was affronted by the unforgiving angles and buildings. He was disoriented and carried off by the terrible rootlessness of the crowds, and he spoke of his unimaginable sadness, of being an "armless poet, lost/in the vomiting crowd." Lorca's vision of the crowd was influenced both by Walt Whitman who, he said, "searched it for solitudes" and by T. S. Eliot who squeezed everything out of it "like a lemon." *Poet in New York* is part "Song of Myself," part "The Waste Land."

The poet in Lorca's urban cycle is an intense flâneur—enraptured, enraged—who wanders all over New York City. Lorca's favorite neighborhood was Harlem, where he heard African American spirituals and jazz tunes that reminded him of Spanish folk music, especially his beloved *canto jondo* ("deep song"), traditional flamenco. His wanderings took him from the Upper West Side, where he lived in a series of residence halls at Columbia University, to Coney Island ("Landscape of the Vomiting Crowd"); he found his way from Riverside Drive to Battery Place ("Landscape of the Urinating Crowd") and over the Brooklyn Bridge ("City Without Sleep"). He was on Wall Street on the day of the stock market crash and afterward claimed to have seen six people commit suicide during Black Tuesday. There he felt, to an unprecedented degree, "the sensation of real death, death without hope." Lorca was staggered by the suffering around him, the greed, the anthropocentrism of urban life, and he responded with a series of phantasmagoric images, such as the opening of his "Nocturne of the Brooklyn Bridge":

> No one sleeps in the sky. No one. No one.
> No one sleeps.
> The creatures of the moon smell and circle their cabins.
> Live iguanas will come to bite the men who don't dream
> and he who flees with broken heart will find on the corners
> the still, incredible crocodile under the tender protest of the
>   stars.

"I have come from the countryside," Lorca said, "and do not believe that man is the most important thing of all." He was dumbfounded by the daily slaughter of animals, which he described as "a river of tender blood." He captured his disgust in "New York (Office and Denunciation)," where he wrote: "Every day in New York, they slaughter/four million ducks,/five million pigs,/two thousand doves for the pleasure of the dying,/a million cows,/a million lambs,/and two million roosters/that leave the sky in splinters." He denounces "the endless trains of milk,/the endless trains of blood," and becomes a bitter prophet who works himself into a frenzy of condemnation and offers himself up as a sacrifice:

No, no. I denounce.
I denounce the conspiracy of those deserted offices
swept clean of agony,
that erase the designs of the forest,
and I offer myself to be eaten by the crushed cows
when their screams fill the valley
where the Hudson gets drunk on oil.

"Being born in Granada," Lorca once said, "has given me a sympathetic understanding of all those who are persecuted — the Gypsy, the black, the Jew, the Moor, which all Grandians have inside them." He identified with those on the edges, the periphery. Lorca was thunderstruck by the racism he found in the New World ("Oh Harlem! Harlem!/There is no anguish compared to your oppressed reds"), and the theme of racial injustice, of social inequity, runs like a current through *Poet in New York*. He wanted to write, as he put it, "*the* poem of the black race in North America," and he struggled to understand, as he later told an interviewer, "a world shameless and cruel enough to divide people by color when in fact color is the sign of God's artistic genius."

The city Lorca discovered on his many solitary walks becomes in his book a prototype of the twentieth-century urban world. Lorca's diagnosis still holds as he inveighs against our hostility to nature, "the painful slavery of both men and machines," the agonizing social injustice, and the indifference to suffering that seems to permeate the very atmosphere. Yet there is also a great exuberance underlying Lorca's nocturnes and morning songs, his furious rambles that took him all over New York City. The testament he left behind is a fierce indictment of the modern world incarnated in city life, but it is also a wildly imaginative and joyously alienated declaration of residence.

—Edward Hirsch

Introduction

Already a well-known poet and dramatist in his native Spain, Federico García Lorca arrived in New York in August 1929, at age thirty-one, in time to witness the collapse of the stock market that sent the city into a tailspin and much of the world into the Great Depression. That October he experienced firsthand the despair of people who had lost everything. He saw the suicides splayed on the sidewalks. He sensed a city on the verge of moral and spiritual collapse. Depressed and grieving over the results of a broken love affair, Lorca had been eager to reach the city and throw himself into its streets. He had read accounts of the grandeur, bustle, and diversity of the great metropolis and seen its images projected on movie screens. What he found had little to do with what he had read or seen. New York was larger and more consuming than any other city he knew. It was abrasive, dirty, caustic, cold, shadowy, and dangerous; in short, it was an analog of hell as terrifying as any depicted in literature or art to that time. All of what he experienced on the streets of the city, however, paled before the horror he felt on Wall Street, where, he wrote in an essay, "rivers of gold arrived from all parts of the earth, and with it death. Nowhere else on earth but there can one feel the total absence of the spirit." Coming to rid himself of grief, he encounters an abundance of grief; coming to witness the power of human endeavor, he finds inhumanity, tragedy, failure.

Seventy years later, those of us who had seen the twin towers of the World Trade Center rise over the cityscape and accepted them, reluctantly, as symbols of New York's vigor and permanence found it difficult to witness how easily they came down, how the raw materials of our daily lives—glass, steel, concrete, and human flesh—could, in the space of two hours, turn to rubble: "Murdered by the sky./Among the forms that move toward the snake/and the forms searching for crystal. . . ." Their weakness was our weakness, their impermanence our impermanence. For weeks after the disaster, smoke and dust filled the air, and the prevailing winds carried them uptown to the Bronx, east toward Brooklyn and Queens, west toward New Jersey. That smoke had the strangest smell of wrecked buildings and decaying bodies, which we tried to avoid by closing our windows, by wearing ineffective felt masks, or by holding handkerchiefs to our faces. New York had received a deep wound and we felt those airplanes reach inside us, crash, and burn through our sun-filled morning again and again:

> The light is buried by noises and chains
> in the obscene challenge of rootless science.
> In the neighborhoods are people who wander unsleeping
> like survivors of a shipwreck of blood.

Seeking solace we read the literature of New York: the poetry of Whitman, the chronicles of José Martí, Hart Crane's "The Bridge," E. B. White's extraordinary essay, "Here Is New York," the myriad novels and plays the city has inspired; and we dove into Ginsberg, Corso, Koch, O'Hara—in short, into the body of work that informs and defines the spiritual fabric of our city. Then we came to García Lorca's *Poet in New York* and saw reflected in this book the range of emotions we ourselves felt and images strangely reminiscent of the ones we witnessed on September 11 and its aftermath.

One afternoon a couple of years later, we realized a new translation of *Poet in New York* was needed that showed the city, not just as it was then but as it became after September 11, riven by tragedy, burdened by rage, humbled by grief. Who would be better suited to the job than two New York poets, neither of whom was a professional translator or scholar but who were for decades (still are) devoted readers of Lorca?

While Lorca could have admitted defeat and returned home soon after his arrival in 1929, instead he confronted the city and in so doing he faced the sources of his grief and the repositories of his fears, a New York transformed into Lorca, a Lorca transformed into New York. As he himself wrote, "I have said a poet in New York, and I should have said, 'New York in a poet.'" Stripped bare, made vulnerable before this new world, Lorca kept his anguish from his family and in frequent letters home he chronicled a time filled with friends and parties, visits and discoveries. But his struggles with New York were real. Through poetry he discovered a way to contain and shape the experience, offering not so much a shield for protection as a way into himself and a conduit through the heartless modern megalopolis. Lorca's journey not only led to some of his finest writing, it also provided him with ways to address personal and social issues that would continue the rest of his short life. He became much less ambivalent about his homosexuality, more accepting of his conflicted but nevertheless deeply held religious faith, and deeply critical of the destructive capacity of unchecked industry and capitalism. Like a performer of *cante jondo*, or deep song, an especially emotive form of flamenco, he ended up struggling with *duende*, that mysterious force that underlies all great art, his own particular *duende* as well as that of the city. As Lorca wrote in "Play and Theory of the *Duende*," *duende* leads neither to victory nor defeat; it is not a protective cloak or a fiery sword. And it certainly is not diversion. It doesn't keep "the lobsters of arsenic" from falling on your head. *Duende* wounds and with the wounding comes creation, the poem "baptizing with dark waters all who behold it."

When Lorca left New York for Cuba in 1930 he was not fleeing *duende*. It had come and gone, perhaps never to return again. In Cuba he found forms of music and dance—we should say forms of living—that were parallel to those he found among the North American blacks in the Harlem he so admired: "Blacks . . . are among the most spiritual and delicate [beings] of that world. Because they believe, because they hope, because they sing, and because they have a truly religious lassitude. . . ." And in those Cuban roots he encountered echoes and convergences of flamenco, of Hispanic notes embedded among African rhythms. As he approached Cuba he asked, "What is this? Once again Spain?

Once again the global Andalusia?" In Cuba he discovered the Spanish *duende* and the African *duende* joined at the hip. Through his experiences in New York, through *duende*, he had discovered himself, wounded and wiser, a fuller man and a greater poet.

The great poets speak to each other, across time and language and they echo each other, not always consciously. To find Lorca's poetic peers we must look to Dante, Blake, Baudelaire, and Eliot. Dante's travels through the Inferno, like Eliot's through the Wasteland, are not unlike Lorca's through New York. His sense of innocence and experience, mediated by the imagination and driven to engage and understand the physical and spiritual world, echoes Blake. And his view of reality in which good and evil are in a continual dance, at times so manic they blur together, brings us to Baudelaire.

Lorca was not in any strict sense a man of politics, a poet of the political. He did not belong to any political party or subscribe to a particular ideology. He was, however, a man of deeply held convictions. From a very early age he felt a special bond to the peasants and gypsies, the common people of his native Andalusia. He witnessed the dire poverty in which they lived and was privy to the sordid conditions under which they functioned daily. For hundreds of years Spain had ignored the backbone of its population, the agrarian poor, who lived away from the centers of culture, such as Madrid and Barcelona. Lorca was a steadfast supporter of the Spanish Republic and in the 1930s, at a time when the republic was being challenged by the Nationalists, who longed for a return of the monarchy, with government support he founded La Barraca, a grass-roots theater project that took classical and contemporary plays, including his own, to all corners of Spain. Such an association, no matter that it was on behalf of Spanish culture, an immense source of pride for all Spaniards despite their political affiliation, was one of the factors that contributed to Lorca's murder.

In July 1936, long after Lorca returned from his trip to New York and Cuba, the tensions between loyalist supporters of the Second Spanish Republic and the Nationalists spilled over into open civil war. The following month Lorca was apprehended by a group of disaffected Nationalists and taken to the village of Víznar, a place notorious as an execution site. At dawn on the nineteenth of August, Lorca, along with a teacher and two anarchist bullfighters, was taken to a place called Fuente Grande and executed.

Why was Lorca killed? Was he shot because he was a poet, because he was a supporter of the republic, because he was a homosexual? Given his fame and the support he received from many people of diverse political beliefs, and considering how well-liked he and his family were in Granada, his murder defies the most ardent attempts at a reasonable explanation. His body was never found and it wasn't until 1986 that a monument was constructed where he is believed to have been murdered. It reads, "In memory of Federico García Lorca and all the victims of the Civil War."

Lorca remains a spirit of wonder and grace over Granada and Andalusia, places he loved deeply. He remains, too, the poet in New York, walking the streets, confronting its clamor, absorbing the city's energy (the urban spirit alive), and offering it all back to us in its horror and stark beauty, its squalor and magnificence, as the incarnation of our paradoxical age.

It was only when we started translating Lorca's *Poet in New York* that our sense of the work of a translator took on a dramatic change, or shift in perspective, because suddenly the goal became how to take the language that Lorca wrote in—which looks remarkably like Spanish but is really a language called Lorca—and render that into a language that looks remarkably like English but remains, again, a language called Lorca.

The need to approximate this language subtlety adds a difficult and complex layer to the work of translating. Lorca wrote into and as part of a culture and tradition, into and of a historical moment, as well as into and of a personal life (physical, emotional, intellectual, spiritual). All of these (and a lot more) are bound inevitably and inextricably into the poetry itself.

Our initial method of translating seemed rather straight-forward, but it's clear that the straightforwardness has some important underlying assumptions. We agreed that each of us would translate every poem on our own. We would do these in small, previously agreed-upon bunches and then exchange these translations. Alternating the poems, each of us would be respon-sible for reconciling the differences between the two versions, a third version thus emerging. We'd then meet to reconcile those reconciliations.

We discovered along the way a lot of things. One was that even though neither of us would characterize ourself in any way as an academic literary scholar, we still needed to do a lot of criti-cal homework, a lot of research about Lorca and *Poet in New York*. The research revealed to us the unusual provenance of the book. Lorca never organized the whole of the collection. It was not published as a single book in his lifetime, nor were a num-ber of the poems that have been included in the collection. There are multiple variations on some of the individual poems and multiple versions with different poems included, excluded, or added as appendices, depending on the editors and transla-tors, of the text we know as *Poet in New York*. As another set of translators, we have also been required to make choices about the text.

In addition to discovering the need for research, we discov-ered that our collaboration prevented us from being sloppy with language, from being imprecise, vague, or clunky, because each of us knew the other was looking over his shoulder. We found new ways to read through Lorca's surreal-like language and mul-tiple ways to read what seemed at first to be easy lines. We learned from Lorca and each other new ways of reading the Spanish lan-guage—words specific to Andalusia and Granada, which are de-fined differently elsewhere. The word *polos*, for example, in the poem "Norma y paraíso de los negros" ("Norm and Paradise of the Blacks") can translate as the poles (North and South). But here things become interesting. *Polo* has a unique meaning in

Andalusia, the region in Spain where Lorca grew up. There it also means a form of traditional music and dance. Given the cultural reference in the title of the poem to Small's Paradise, a Harlem Renaissance jazz club, this suggested to us that, between the form of music and dance and the nightclub we could translate *polos* not as *poles*, but as *flamenco* because of the strength it gave to the image of the line: "the lying moon of flamenco" as opposed to "the lying moon of poles." And this is how we initially translated it. We liked the fact that it would have been an unusual translation. It was a translation we could have argued made sense save for one key fact: Lorca had not written *el polo* but *los polos*. This plural (the *flamencos?*) could only lead us back to the *poles* of north and south. And poles, after a lot of thinking, is what we realized made the most sense.

Another example is Lorca's use of the word *chino*, a common one in *Poet in New York*. *Chino* can refer to a Chinese man. In the feminine *china* can refer to a Chinese woman. But a *naranja china* is also a small juicy orange. The word *chino* can also indicate a kind of aural cacophony. It can refer to someone who is deceitful, a trickster. And, in Granada, the capital of Lorca's Andalusía, a *china* is a small stone used in paving streets. Context left us with the most obvious, the Chinese man (or *Chinaman*, with all the negative connotations the word carries from Spanish into English), but the other meanings were important in our thinking because they were meanings we knew Lorca knew.

In collaborating, we also found it critical not only to check each other for accuracy but for liberty—when one of us chose to experiment with Lorca, to go over the top, as it were, usually when it seemed there was no other alternative, the other was there to question the experiment. Was this really Lorca? Was this beyond meaning and new interpretation? If interpretation, was it legitimate and necessary interpretation? The presence of the collaborator thus gave us each greater confidence to experiment, to play; in fact, to discover different, and often better ways to write Lorca into English.

This last part of our working method also made it clear how important being poets ourselves was to this particular task of translation. Moving through drafts, thinking out questions of Lorca and his project, led us to secondary and significant ways to solve translation issues. After wondering what Lorca was trying to do, the later phases of our work continued to have the wondering of translators but it added the wondering of poets. For both of us a new and useful question became not simply what was Lorca doing but what would each of us, as a poet, do? How would we address the poetic problems Lorca presented? This part of the collaboration left both of us feeling some trepidation because it meant that the Medina/Statman collaboration had become the making finally of something that Lorca did not actually write. Doing this we found ourselves playing with Lorca's forms, with his repetitions, his arrangements of sequence and line. At times we found the need to make the poems leaner than the original, with less of Lorca's overwhelming language and cadences in Spanish. All this play, this erasure, has seemed necessary to retain the feeling, the power, the music of Lorca's work.

This was obviously one of the more creative and sensitive parts of the collaboration. Here were two poets translating, writing, re-writing a poem, a book of poems, an activity that, to cite Robert Lowell, in some way functions as an imitation of another poet. Here were two poets translating, writing, rewriting a book of poems that, to cite Gregory Rabassa, will become the version for numerous (we hope) other readers. In giving ourselves leave to be more than a combination dictionary/grammar/usage text, we demanded of ourselves a great deal of humility and a bit of hubris, demanded the necessity of allowing the poetic ego to work and the necessity to also say no to that very ego. Because, in thinking about how *I* as a poet or how *we* as poets would do this, we were also responsible for remembering that often that very question, the one framed by the *I* or the *we*, while satisfying to think about, may also be irrelevant to the poem we were translating. As such, translating Lorca, arguably the greatest Spanish poet of the twentieth century, and *Poet in New York*, arguably his greatest book of poems, has required reverence and irreverence, caution and wildness, timidity and chutzpah.

To read *Poet in New York* in the version we offer here is to read not prophecy but chronicle, not the future but the present. We have lost the New York City of September 10, 2001. What we gained is a New York in some ways wiser, sadder, and perhaps better able to deal with both triumph and tragedy. We cannot quantify grief, nor can we quantify hope. They are not found in mourning prayers or in hate, not in the call to arms or in prejudice, not in money or fast cars or the most glittering jewels or the tallest buildings or the smartest books. These are ancient lessons Lorca learned well in New York, and we, lulled into complacency by our collective wealth, forgot and relearned in a nightmare of fire and ash. To read this book now is to see Lorca's eyes — eyes of a child — staring from the anonymous grave into which he was thrown after his murder and to hear the black sounds of *duende* carried by the Spanish breeze above our buildings and streets to a place where true grief and hope, twin sisters, reside.

Poeta en Nueva York / Poet in New York

A BEBÉ Y CARLOS MORLA
Los poemas de este libro están escritos en la ciudad de Nueva
York el año 1929–1930, en que el poeta vivió como estudiante en
Columbia University.

F.G.L.

TO BEBÉ AND CARLOS MORLA
The poems of this book were written in the city of New York during
the year 1929–1930, in which the poet lived as a student at
Columbia University.

F.G.L.

I
Poemas de la soledad
en Columbia University

Furia color de amor,
amor color de olvido.

—*Luis Cernuda*

I
Poems of Solitude
at Columbia University

Fury, the color of love,
love, the color of forgetting.

—*Luis Cernuda*

VUELTA DE PASEO

Asesinado por el cielo,
entre las formas que van hacia la sierpe
y las formas que buscan el cristal,
dejaré crecer mis cabellos.

Con el árbol de muñones que no canta
y el niño con el blanco rostro de huevo.

Con los animalitos de cabeza rota
y el agua harapienta de los pies secos.

Con todo lo que tiene cansancio sordomudo
y mariposa ahogada en el tintero.

Tropezando con mi rostro distinto de cada día.
¡Asesinado por el cielo!

BACK FROM A WALK

Murdered by the sky.
Among the forms that move toward the snake
and the forms searching for crystal
I will let my hair grow.

With the limbless tree that cannot sing
and the boy with the white egg face.

With the broken-headed animals
and the ragged water of dry feet.

With all that is tired, deaf-mute,
and a butterfly drowned in an inkwell.

Stumbling onto my face, different every day.
Murdered by the sky!

Federico García Lorca / 5

1910

(Intermedio)

Aquellos ojos míos de mil novecientos diez
no vieron enterrar a los muertos,
ni la feria de ceniza del que llora por la madrugada,
ni el corazón que tiembla arrinconado como un caballito de mar.

Aquellos ojos míos de mil novecientos diez
vieron la blanca pared donde orinaban las niñas,
el hocico del toro, la seta venenosa
y una luna incomprensible que iluminaba por los rincones
los pedazos de limón seco bajo el negro duro de las botellas.

Aquellos ojos míos en el cuello de la jaca,
en el seno traspasado de Santa Rosa dormida,
en los tejados del amor, con gemidos y frescas manos,
en un jardín donde los gatos se comían a las ranas.

Desván donde el polvo viejo congrega estatuas y musgos,
cajas que guardan silencio de cangrejos devorados
en el sitio donde el sueño tropezaba con su realidad.
Allí mis pequeños ojos.

No preguntarme nada. He visto que las cosas
cuando buscan su curso encuentran su vacío.
Hay un dolor de huecos por el aire sin gente
y en mis ojos criaturas vestidas ¡sin desnudo!

New York, agosto 1929

1910

(Interlude)

My eyes in 1910
never saw the dead being buried,
or the ashen festival of a man weeping at dawn,
or the heart that trembles cornered like a sea horse.

My eyes in 1910
saw the white wall where girls urinated,
the bull's muzzle, the poisonous mushroom,
and a meaningless moon in the corners
that lit up pieces of dry lemon under the hard black of bottles.

My eyes on the pony's neck,
in the pierced breast of a sleeping Saint Rose,
on the rooftops of love, with whimpers and cool hands,
in a garden where the cats ate frogs.

Attic where old dust gathers statues and moss,
boxes keeping the silence of devoured crabs
in a place where sleep stumbled onto its reality.
There my small eyes.

Don't ask me anything. I've seen that things
find their void when they search for direction.
There is a sorrow of holes in the unpeopled air
and in my eyes clothed creatures—undenuded!

New York, August 1929

FÁBULA Y RUEDA DE LOS TRES AMIGOS

Enrique,
Emilio,
Lorenzo,

estaban los tres helados:
Enrique por el mundo de las camas;
Emilio por el mundo de los ojos y las heridas de las manos;
Lorenzo por el mundo de las universidades sin tejados.

Lorenzo,
Emilio,
Enrique,

estaban los tres quemados:
Lorenzo por el mundo de las hojas y las bolas de billar;
Emilio por el mundo de la sangre y los alfileres blancos;
Enrique por el mundo de los muertos y los periódicos
    abandonados.

Lorenzo,

Emilio,
Enrique,
estaban los tres enterrados:
Lorenzo en un seno de Flora;
Emilio en la yerta ginebra que se olvida en el vaso;
Enrique en la hormiga, en el mar y en los ojos vacíos
    de los pájaros.

FABLE AND ROUND OF THE THREE FRIENDS

Enrique,
Emilio,
Lorenzo,

the three of them frozen:
Enrique by the world of beds;
Emilio by the world of eyes and wounded hands;
Lorenzo by the world of roofless universities.

Lorenzo,
Emilio,
Enrique,

the three of them burned:
Lorenzo by the world of leaves and billiard balls;
Emilio by the world of blood and white pins;
Enrique by the world of the dead and abandoned
        newspapers.

Lorenzo,

Emilio,
Enrique,
the three of them buried:
Lorenzo in one of Flora's breasts;
Emilio in the dead gin forgotten in the glass;
Enrique in the ant, the sea, and the empty eyes
        of birds.

Lorenzo,

Emilio,
Enrique,
fueron los tres en mis manos
tres montañas chinas,
tres sombras de caballo,
tres paisajes de nieve y una cabaña de azucenas
por los palomares donde la luna se pone plana bajo el gallo.

Uno

y uno
y uno,
estaban los tres momificados,
con las moscas del invierno,
con los tinteros que orina el perro y desprecia el vilano,
con la brisa que hiela el corazón de todas las madres,
por los blancos derribos de Júpiter donde meriendan muerte
    los borrachos.

Tres

y dos
y uno,
los vi perderse llorando y cantando
por un huevo de gallina,
por la noche que enseñaba su esqueleto de tabaco,
por mi dolor lleno de rostros y punzantes esquirlas de
    luna
por mi alegría de ruedas dentadas y látigos,
por mi pecho turbado por las palomas,
por mi muerte desierta con un solo paseante equivocado.

Lorenzo,

Emilio,
Enrique,
the three in my hands were
three Chinese mountains,
three shadows of a horse,
three landscapes of snow and a cabin of white lilies
by the pigeon coops where the moon lies flat under the rooster.

One

and one
and one,
the three of them mummified,
with the flies of winter,
with the inkwells the dog pisses and the thistle despises,
with the breeze that freezes the heart of all the mothers,
by the white ruins of Jupiter where drunks snack
        on death.

Three

and two
and one,
I saw them disappear, crying and singing
into a hen's egg,
into the night that showed its skeleton of tobacco,
into my sorrow full of faces and piercing bone splinters of
        moon,
into my happiness of whips and notched wheels,
into my breast troubled by pigeons,
into my deserted death with one mistaken wanderer.

Federico García Lorca / 11

Yo había matado la quinta luna
y bebían agua por las fuentes los abanicos y los aplausos.
Tibia leche encerrada de las recién paridas
agitaba las rosas con un largo dolor blanco.
Enrique,
Emilio,
Lorenzo.

Diana es dura,
pero a veces tiene los pechos nublados.
Puede la piedra blanca latir en la sangre del ciervo
y el ciervo puede soñar por los ojos de un caballo.

Cuando se hundieron las formas puras
bajo el cri cri de las margaritas,
comprendí que me habían asesinado.
Recorrieron los cafés y los cementerios y las iglesias,
abrieron los toneles y los armarios,
destrozaron tres esqueletos para arrancar sus dientes de oro.
Ya no me encontraron.
¿No me encontraron?
No. No me encontraron.
Pero se supo que la sexta luna huyó torrente arriba,
y que el mar recordó ¡de pronto!
los nombres de todos sus ahogados.

I had killed the fifth moon
and the fans and the applause drank water from the fountains.
Hidden away, the warm milk of newborn girls,
shook the roses with a long white sorrow.
Enrique,
Emilio,
Lorenzo,

Diana is hard,
but sometimes she has breasts of clouds.
The white stone can beat in the blood of a deer
and the deer can dream through the eyes of a horse.

When the pure forms sank
under the *cri cri* of daisies
I understood they had murdered me.
They searched the cafés and the graveyards and churches,
they opened the wine casks and wardrobes,
they destroyed three skeletons to pull out their gold teeth.
Still they couldn't find me.
They couldn't?
No. They couldn't.
But they learned the sixth moon fled against the torrent,
and the sea remembered, suddenly,
the names of all her drowned.

TU INFANCIA EN MENTON

Sí, tu niñez ya fábula de fuentes.
> —Jorge Guillén

Sí, tu niñez ya fábula de fuentes.
El tren y la mujer que llena el cielo.
Tu soledad esquiva en los hoteles
y tu máscara pura de otro signo.
Es la niñez del mar y tu silencio
donde los sabios vidrios se quebraban.
Es tu yerta ignorancia donde estuvo
mi torso limitado por el fuego.
Norma de amor te di, hombre de Apolo,
llanto con ruiseñor enajenado,
pero, pasto de ruina, te afilabas
para los breves sueños indecisos.
Pensamiento de enfrente, luz de ayer,
índices y señales del acaso.
Tu cintura de arena sin sosiego
atiende solo rastros que no escalan.
Pero yo he de buscar por los rincones
tu alma tibia sin ti que no te entiende,
con el dolor de Apolo detenido
con que he roto la máscara que llevas.
Allí, león, allí furia del cielo,
te dejaré pacer en mis mejillas;
allí, caballo azul de mi locura,
pulso de nebulosa y minutero,
he de buscar las piedras de alacranes
y los vestidos de tu madre niña,
llanto de media noche y paño roto
que quitó luna de la sien del muerto.
Sí, tu niñez ya fábula de fuentes.

YOUR INFANCY IN MENTON

Yes, your childhood now a fable of fountains.
                    —Jorge Guillén

Yes, your childhood now a fable of fountains.
The train and the woman filling the sky.
Your shy solitude in the hotels
and your pure mask of another sign.
It is the sea's childhood and your silence
where the wise windows were breaking.
It is your stiff ignorance where
my torso was limited by fire.
I gave you the norm of love, man of Apollo,
the lament of a crazed nightingale,
but, pasture of ruin, you sharpened yourself
for brief, indecisive dreams.
Thought head on, light of yesterday,
indices and signs of what may be.
Your waist of restless sand
follows only trails that never rise.
But without you your warm soul
fails to understand I must search
the corners of a halted Apollo
that I've used to break the mask you wear.
There, lion, fury of heaven,
I will let you graze on my cheeks;
there, blue horse of my madness,
pulse of nebula and minute hand,
I must search for scorpion stones
and your mother's childhood clothes,
midnight lament and torn cloth
that wiped the moon from the dead man's temple.
Yes, your childhood now a fable of fountains.

Federico García Lorca / 15

Alma extraña de mi hueco de venas,
te he de buscar pequeña y sin raíces.
¡Amor de siempre, amor, amor de nunca!
¡Oh, sí! Yo quiero. ¡Amor, amor! Dejadme.
No me tapen la boca los que buscan
espigas de Saturno por la nieve
o castran animales por un cielo,
clínica y selva de la anatomía.
Amor, amor, amor. Niñez del mar.
Tu alma tibia sin ti que no te entiende.
Amor, amor, un vuelo de la corza
por el pecho sin fin de la blancura.
Y tu niñez, amor, y tu niñez.
El tren y la mujer que llena el cielo.
Ni tú, ni yo, ni el aire, ni las hojas.
Sí, tu niñez ya fábula de fuentes.

Strange soul of the space in my veins,
I must search for you, small and rootless.
Love of always, love of never!
Oh, yes! I want. Love. Let me be.
Don't cover my mouth, you
who search for Saturn's seed in the snow
or castrate animals in the sky,
clinic and jungle of anatomy.
Love, love. Childhood of the sea.
Without you your warm soul fails to understand you.
Love, a doe's flight
through the endless breast of whiteness.
And your childhood, love, and childhood.
The train and the woman filling the sky.
Not you, not I, not air, not leaves.
Yes, your childhood now a fable of fountains.

II
Los Negros

Para Ángel del Río

II
The Blacks

For Ángel del Río

NORMA Y PARAÍSO DE LOS NEGROS

Odian la sombra del pájaro
sobre el pleamar de la blanca mejilla
y el conflicto de luz y viento
en el salón de la nieve fría.

Odian la flecha sin cuerpo,
el pañuelo exacto de la despedida,
la aguja que mantiene presión y rosa
en el gramíneo rubor de la sonrisa.

Aman el azul desierto,
las vacilantes expresiones bovinas,
la mentirosa luna de los polos,
la danza curva del agua en la orilla.

Con la ciencia del tronco y del rastro
llenan de nervios luminosos la arcilla
y patinan lúbricos por aguas y arenas
gustando la amarga frescura de su milenaria saliva.

Es por el azul crujiente,
azul sin un gusano ni una huella dormida,
donde los huevos de avestruz quedan eternos
y deambulan intactas las lluvias bailarinas.

Es por el azul sin historia,
azul de una noche sin temor de día,
azul donde el desnudo del viento va quebrando
los camellos sonámbulos de las nubes vacías.

NORM AND PARADISE OF THE BLACKS

They hate the shadow of the bird
over the high water of the white cheek
and the conflict of light and wind
in the salon of the cold snow.

They hate the bodiless arrow,
the precise handkerchief's farewell,
the needle that keeps the pressure and the rose
in the cereal blush of the smile.

They love the blue desert,
the swaying bovine expressions,
the lying moon of the poles,
the water's curved dance at the shore.

With the science of tree trunk and street market
they fill the clay with luminous nerves
and lewdly skate on waters and sands
tasting the bitter freshness of their millennial spit.

It's through the crackling blue,
blue without worm or a sleeping footprint,
where the ostrich eggs remain eternal
and the dancing rains wander untouched.

It's through the blue without history,
blue of a night without fear of day,
blue where the nude of the wind goes splitting
the sleepwalking camels of the empty clouds.

Es allí donde sueñan los torsos bajo la gula de la hierba.
Allí los corales empapan la desesperación de la tinta,
los durmientes borran sus perfiles bajo la madeja de los
    caracoles
y queda el hueco de la danza sobre las últimas cenizas.

It's there where the torsos dream under the gluttony of grass.
There the corals soak the ink's despair,
the sleepers erase their profiles under the skein of
     snails
and the space of the dance remains over the final ashes.

EL REY DE HARLEM

Con una cuchara,
arrancaba los ojos a los cocodrilos
y golpeaba el trasero de los monos.
Con una cuchara.

Fuego de siempre dormía en los pedernales
y los escarabajos borrachos de anís
olvidaban el musgo de las aldeas.

Aquel viejo cubierto de setas
iba al sitio donde lloraban los negros
mientras crujía la cuchara del rey
y llegaban los tanques de agua podrida.

Las rosas huían por los filos
de las últimas curvas del aire,
y en los montones de azafrán
los niños machacaban pequeñas ardillas
con un rubor de frenesí manchado.

Es preciso cruzar los puentes
y llegar al rubor negro
para que el perfume de pulmón
nos golpee las sienes con su vestido
de caliente piña.

Es preciso matar al rubio vendedor de aguardiente,
a todos los amigos de la manzana y de la arena,
y es necesario dar con los puños cerrados
a las pequeñas judías que tiemblan llenas de burbujas,
para que el rey de Harlem cante con su muchedumbre,

THE KING OF HARLEM

With a spoon
he scooped out the eyes of crocodiles
and beat the monkeys' behinds.
With a spoon.

Fire of always slept in the flint
and the scarabs drunk on *anís*
forgot the moss of the villages.

That old man covered with mushrooms
went to the place where the blacks were crying
while the king's spoon rang
and the tanks of rotten water arrived.

The roses fled down the edges
of the last curves of air,
and on mounds of saffron
children crushed small squirrels
in a flush of stained frenzy.

One must cross the bridges
and arrive at the black shame
so that the lung's perfume
hits our temples with its clothing
of hot pineapple.

One must kill the blond seller of firewater,
kill all the friends of street and sand
and one must punch
the small Jewish women who tremble full of bubbles,
so the king of Harlem sings with the crowd,

para que los cocodrilos duerman en largas filas
bajo el amianto de la luna,
y para que nadie dude de la infinita belleza
de los plumeros, los ralladores, los cobres y las cacerolas
    de las cocinas.

¡Ay Harlem! ¡Ay Harlem! ¡Ay Harlem!
¡No hay angustia comparable a tus rojos oprimidos,
a tu sangre estremecida dentro del eclipse oscuro,
a tu violencia granate sordomuda en la penumbra,
a tu gran rey prisionero con un traje de conserje!

                    *

Tenía la noche una hendidura y quietas salamandras de
    marfil.
Las muchachas americanas
llevaban niños y monedas en el vientre,
y los muchachos se desmayaban en la cruz del desperezo.

Ellos son.
Ellos son los que beben el whisky de plata junto a los volcanes
y tragan pedacitos de corazón por las heladas montañas del oso.

Aquella noche el rey de Harlem,
con una durísima cuchara
arrancaba los ojos a los cocodrilos
y golpeaba el trasero de los monos.
Con una cuchara.
Los negros lloraban confundidos
entre paraguas y soles de oro,
los mulatos estiraban gomas, ansiosos de llegar al torso
    blanco,
y el viento empañaba espejos
y quebraba las venas de los bailarines.

Negros, Negros, Negros, Negros.

so the crocodiles sleep in long lines
under the asbestos of the moon,
and no one doubts the infinite beauty
of the feather dusters, the graters, the copper pots and pans of
    the kitchen.

Oh Harlem! Harlem!
There is no anguish compared to your oppressed reds,
to your blood shaken inside the dark eclipse,
to your garnet violence, deaf and mute in the shadows,
to your great prisoner king in his janitor's uniform.

*

The night had a crack and quiet salamanders
    of ivory.
The American girls
carried children and coins in the belly
and the boys fainted stretched on the cross.

They are.
They are the ones who drink silver whiskey next to volcanoes
and swallow bits of heart on the frozen mountain of bear.

That night the king of Harlem
with a very hard spoon
scooped out the eyes of the crocodiles
and beat the monkeys' behinds.
With a spoon.
The blacks wept, confused
between umbrellas and suns of gold,
the mulattos stretched rubber bands, wanting to reach the
    white torso,
and the wind fogged mirrors
and broke the veins of the dancers.

Blacks.

La sangre no tiene puertas en vuestra noche boca arriba.
No hay rubor. Sangre furiosa por debajo de las pieles,
viva en la espina del puñal y en el pecho de los paisajes,
bajo las pinzas y las retamas de la celeste luna
    de cáncer.

Sangre que busca por mil caminos muertes enharinadas y
    ceniza de nardo,
cielos yertos en declive, donde las colonias de planetas
rueden por las playas con los objetos abandonados.

Sangre que mira lenta con el rabo del ojo,
hecha de espartos exprimidos, néctares de subterráneos.
Sangre que oxida el alisio descuidado en una huella
y disuelve a las mariposas en los cristales de la ventana.

Es la sangre que viene, que vendrá
por los tejados y azoteas, por todas partes,
para quemar la clorofila de las mujeres rubias,
para gemir al pie de las camas ante el insomnio de los lavabos
y estrellarse en una aurora de tabaco y bajo amarillo.

Hay que huir,
huir por las esquinas y encerrarse en los últimos pisos,
porque el tuétano del bosque penetrará por las rendijas
para dejar en vuestra carne una leve huella de eclipse
y una falsa tristeza de guante desteñido y rosa química.

                    *

Es por el silencio sapientísimo
cuando los camareros y los cocineros y los que limpian con la
    lengua
las heridas de los millonarios
buscan al rey por las calles o en los ángulos del salitre.

Blood has no doors in your night, face up.
There is no shame. Furious blood under the skin
alive in the dagger's spine and in the breast of the landscapes,
under the clamps and small yellow flowers of the celestial
     moon of cancer.

Blood that seeks death down a thousand roads,
death covered with flour and the ash of fragrant weeds,
rigid skies sloping where the colonies of planets
roll down to beaches with abandoned objects.

Blood that looks slowly out the corner of its eye,
made of crushed grass, underground nectars.
Blood that rusts the careless winds in a footprint
and dissolves butterflies on the window glass.

It's the blood that comes, that will come,
down flat and tiled roofs everywhere
to burn the chlorophyll of blonde women,
to moan at the foot of the beds before the sinks' insomnia,
and crash in a dawn of tobacco and yellow haze.

One must flee,
flee past corners and hide in the highest floors,
because the forest's marrow will penetrate the cracks
to leave on your flesh the faint footprint of an eclipse
and the false sadness of a faded glove and a chemical rose.

                          *

It's in the wisest silence,
that's when the waiters and cooks and those who clean with
     their tongues
the wounds of the millionaires
search for the king in the streets or in the angles of saltpeter.

Un viento sur de madera, oblicuo en el negro fango,
escupe a las barcas rotas y se clava puntillas en los hombros;
un viento sur que lleva
colmillos, girasoles, alfabetos
y una pila de Volta con avispas ahogadas.

El olvido estaba expresado por tres gotas de tinta sobre el
      monóculo;
el amor, por un solo rostro invisible a flor de piedra.
Médulas y corolas componían sobre las nubes
un desierto de tallos sin una sola rosa.

                              *

A la izquierda, a la derecha, por el Sur y por el Norte,
se levanta el muro imposible
para el topo y la aguja del agua.
No busquéis, negros, su grieta
para hallar la máscara infinita.
Buscad el gran sol del centro
hechos una piña zumbadora.
El sol que se desliza por los bosques
seguro de no encontrar una ninfa,
el sol que destruye números y no ha cruzado nunca un sueño,
el tatuado sol que baja por el río
y muge seguido de caimanes.

Negros, Negros, Negros, Negros.

Jamás sierpe, ni cebra, ni mula
palidecieron al morir.
El leñador no sabe cuándo expiran
los clamorosos árboles que corta.
Aguardad bajo la sombra vegetal de vuestro rey
a que cicutas y cardos y ortigas turben postreras azoteas.

A south wind of wood, slanting in the black mud,
spits at the broken barges and hammers nails into its shoulders;
a south wind carrying
fangs, sunflowers, alphabets,
and a battery with drowned wasps.

What we forgot was expressed by three drops of ink on the
     monocle,
love by a single invisible face from the stone's level.
Medullas and corollas composed above the clouds
a desert of stalks without a single rose.

*

To the left, to the right, to the south and the north
an impossible wall goes up
for the mole and the needle of water.
Don't look, blacks, in its crevice
to find the infinite mask.
Look for the great sun of the center.
Turn into a buzzing hive.
The sun slides through the forest
sure not to find the nymph,
the sun that destroys numbers and never has crossed a dream,
the tattooed sun that goes to the river
and moans pursued by caimans.

Blacks.

Never did serpent or zebra or mule
pale before dying.
The woodsman doesn't know when the clamorous trees
he cuts down die.
Wait under the vegetable shadow of your king
till hemlock, thistle, and nettle trouble the farthest roofs.

Entonces, negros, entonces, entonces,
podréis besar con frenesí las ruedas de las bicicletas,
poner parejas de microscopios en las cuevas de las ardillas
y danzar al fin, sin duda, mientras las flores erizadas
asesinan a nuestro Moisés casi en los juncos del cielo.

¡Ay, Harlem disfrazada!
¡Ay, Harlem, amenazada por un gentío de trajes sin cabeza!
Me llega tu rumor,
me llega tu rumor atravesando troncos y ascensores,
a través de láminas grises,
donde flotan tus automóviles cubiertos de dientes,
a través de los caballos muertos y los crímenes diminutos,
a través de tu gran rey desesperado,
cuyas barbas llegan al mar.

Then, blacks, then,
you can kiss in a frenzy the bicycle wheels,
place pairs of microscopes in the nests of squirrels,
and dance at last, no doubt, while the bristling flowers
murder our Moses close to the rushes of heaven.

Oh Harlem disguised!
Oh Harlem, threatened by a crowd of headless suits!
Your rumbling comes to me,
your rumbling comes through trunks and elevators,
through layers of gray
where your cars float covered by teeth,
through dead horses and small crimes,
through your great desperate king,
whose beard reaches the sea.

IGLESIA ABANDONADA

(Balada de la Gran Guerra)

Yo tenía un hijo que se llamaba Juan.
Yo tenía un hijo.
Se perdió por los arcos un viernes de todos los muertos.
Le vi jugar en las últimas escaleras de la misa
y echaba un cubito de hojalata en el corazón del sacerdote.
He golpeado los ataúdes. ¡Mi hijo! ¡Mi hijo! ¡Mi hijo!
Saqué una pata de gallina por detrás de la luna y luego
comprendí que mi niña era un pez
por donde se alejan las carretas.
Yo tenía una niña.
Yo tenía un pez muerto bajo las cenizas de los incensarios.
Yo tenía un mar. ¿De qué? ¡Dios mío! ¡Un mar!
Subí a tocar las campanas, pero las frutas tenían gusanos
y las cerillas apagadas
se comían los trigos de la primavera.
Yo vi la transparente cigüeña de alcohol
mondar las negras cabezas de los soldados agonizantes
y vi las cabañas de goma
donde giraban las copas llenas de lágrimas.
En las anémonas del ofertorio te encontraré, ¡corazón mío!,
cuando el sacerdote levante la mula y el buey con sus fuertes
    brazos
para espantar los sapos nocturnos que rondan los helados
    paisajes del cáliz.
Yo tenía un hijo que era un gigante,
pero los muertos son más fuertes y saben devorar pedazos de
    cielo.

ABANDONED CHURCH

(Ballad of the Great War)

I had a son named Juan.
I had a son.
He was lost through the arches on the Friday of the dead.
I saw him play on the final ladders of the mass
and he tossed a small tin can into the priest's heart.
I have pounded on the coffins. My son! My son!
I took out a hen's foot from behind the moon and then
I understood my daughter was a fish
into which the wagons retreat.
I had a daughter.
I had a dead fish under the censer's ashes.
I had a sea. Of what? My God! A sea!
I rose to ring the bells but the fruit had worms
and the blown-out tapers
ate the spring wheat.
I saw the transparent stork of alcohol
cleanse the blackened heads of agonizing soldiers
and I saw the rubber cabins
where goblets twirled full of tears.
In the anemones of the offertory I'll find you, my heart,
when the priest raises the mule and the ox on his strong arms
to chase away the nocturnal frogs surrounding the frozen
        landscape of the chalice.
I had a son who was a giant,
but the dead are stronger and know how to devour pieces of
        sky.

Si mi niño hubiera sido un oso,
yo no temería el sigilo de los caimanes,
ni hubiese visto el mar amarrado a los árboles
para ser fornicado y herido por el tropel de los regimientos.
¡Si mi niño hubiera sido un oso!
Me envolveré sobre esta lona dura para no sentir el frío de los
    musgos.
Sé muy bien que me darán una manga o la corbata;
pero en el centro de la misa yo romperé el timón y entonces
vendrá a la piedra la locura de pingüinos y gaviotas
que harán decir a los que duermen y a los que cantan por las
    esquinas:
él tenía un hijo.
¡Un hijo! ¡Un hijo! ¡Un hijo
que no era más que suyo, porque era su hijo!
¡Su hijo! ¡Su hijo! ¡Su hijo!

If my son had been a bear,
I would not fear the secrecy of caimans
or see the sea tied to the trees
to be raped and wounded by the pounding regiments.
If my son had been a bear!
I'll wrap myself in this hard canvas not to feel the moss's cold.
I know well they'll give me a sleeve, a tie;
but in the center of the mass I'll break the helm and then
there will come to the stone the madness of penguins and gulls
who will force those sleeping and singing in corners to say:
He had a son!
A son! A son
who was only his, because he was!
His son! His son!

III
Calles y sueños

A Rafael R. Rapún

Un pájaro de papel en el pecho
dice que el tiempo de los besos no ha llegado.
—Vicente Aleixandre

III
Streets and Dreams

To Rafael R. Rapún

A paper bird in the breast
says the time of kisses has not arrived.
                    —*Vicente Aleixandre*

DANZA DE LA MUERTE

El mascarón. ¡Mirad el mascarón!
¡Cómo viene del África a New York!

Se fueron los árboles de la pimienta,
los pequeños botones de fósforo.
Se fueron los camellos de carne desgarrada
y los valles de luz que el cisne levantaba con el pico.

Era el momento de las cosas secas,
de la espiga en el ojo y el gato laminado,
del óxido de hierro de los grandes puentes
y el definitivo silencio del corcho.

Era la gran reunión de los animales muertos,
traspasados por las espadas de la luz;
la alegría eterna del hipopótamo con las pezuñas de ceniza
y de la gacela con una siempreviva en la garganta.

En la marchita soledad sin honda
el abollado mascarón danzaba.
Medio lado del mundo era de arena,
mercurio y sol dormido el otro medio.

El mascarón. ¡Mirad el mascarón!
¡Arena, caimán y miedo sobre Nueva York!

*

Desfiladeros de cal aprisionaban un cielo vacío
donde sonaban las voces de los que mueren bajo el guano.
Un cielo mondado y puro, idéntico a sí mismo,
con el bozo y lirio agudo de sus montañas invisibles,

DANCE OF DEATH

The mask, look at the mask!
How it comes from Africa to New York!

The pepper trees left,
the small buds of phosphorus.
The flesh-torn camels left
and the valleys of light the swan lifted with its beak.

It was the moment of dry things,
of the wheat stalk in the eye and the laminated cat,
of the rusted iron of the great bridges
and the ultimate silence of cork.

It was the great reunion of dead animals,
pierced by swords of light;
the eternal joy of the hippopotamus with its hooves of ash
and of the gazelle with the everlasting flower in its throat.

In the faded solitude without a sling
the dented mask was dancing.
Half the world was sand,
the other half mercury and sleeping sun.

The mask, look at the mask!
Sand, caiman, and fear over Nueva York!

*

Canyons of lime imprisoned an empty sky
where the voices of those dying under guano sounded.
A sky cleansed and pure, identical to itself,
soft down and sharp lily of its invisible mountains

acabó con los más leves tallitos del canto
y se fue al diluvio empaquetado de la savia,
a través del descanso de los últimos desfiles,
levantando con el rabo pedazos de espejo.

Cuando el chino lloraba en el tejado
sin encontrar el desnudo de su mujer
y el director del banco observaba el manómetro
que mide el cruel silencio de la moneda,
el mascarón llegaba a Wall Street.

No es extraño para la danza
este columbario que pone los ojos amarillos.
De la esfinge a la caja de caudales hay un hilo tenso
que atraviesa el corazón de todos los niños pobres.
El ímpetu primitivo baila con el ímpetu mecánico,
ignorantes en su frenesí de la luz original.
Porque si la rueda olvida su fórmula,
ya puede cantar desnuda con las manadas de caballos;
y si una llama quema los helados proyectos,
el cielo tendrá que huir ante el tumulto de las ventanas.

No es extraño este sitio para la danza, yo lo digo.
El mascarón bailará entre columnas de sangre y de números,
entre huracanes de oro y gemidos de obreros parados
que aullarán, noche oscura, por tu tiempo sin luces,
¡oh salvaje Norteamérica!, ¡oh impúdica!, ¡oh salvaje,
tendida en la frontera de la nieve!

El mascarón. ¡Mirad el mascarón!
¡Qué ola de fango y luciérnaga sobre Nueva York!

*

destroyed the slightest stems of song
and went to the deluge dense with sap
through the pause of the final parades,
lifting pieces of mirror with its tail.

When the Chinaman cried on the roof
without finding the nude of his wife
and the bank director watched the pressure gauge
that measures the cruel silence of coins,
the mask arrived on Wall Street.

It isn't foreign to the dance
this columbarium that yellows the eyes.
From the sphinx to the vault there is a tense thread
that pierces the heart of all poor children.
The primitive drive dances with the mechanical drive,
ignorant in their frenzy of original light.
Because if the wheel forgets its formula
it still can sing nude with herds of horses:
and if a flame burns the frozen plans,
the sky will have to flee before the tumult of the windows.

This place isn't foreign to the dance, I say it.
The mask will dance between columns of blood and numbers,
between hurricanes of gold and moans of idled workers,
who will howl, dark night, for your time without lights.
O savage North America. O impudent and savage,
lying on the frontier of snow!

The mask, look at the mask!
The wave of mud and fireflies over New York!

*

Yo estaba en la terraza luchando con la luna.
Enjambres de ventanas acribillaban un muslo de la noche.
En mis ojos bebían las dulces vacas de los cielos.
Y las brisas de largos remos
golpeaban los cenicientos cristales de Broadway.

La gota de sangre buscaba la luz de la yema del astro
para fingir una muerta semilla de manzana.
El aire de la llanura, empujado por los pastores,
temblaba con un miedo de molusco sin concha.

Pero no son los muertos los que bailan,
estoy seguro.
Los muertos están embebidos, devorando sus propias manos.
Son los otros los que bailan con el mascarón y su vihuela;
son los otros, los borrachos de plata, los hombres fríos,
los que crecen en el cruce de los muslos y llamas duras,
los que buscan la lombriz en el paisaje de las escaleras,
los que beben en el banco lágrimas de niña muerta
o los que comen por las esquinas diminutas pirámides del alba.

¡Que no baile el Papa!
¡No, que no baile el Papa!
Ni el Rey,
ni el millonario de dientes azules,
ni las bailarinas secas de las catedrales,
ni constructores, ni esmeraldas, ni locos, ni sodomitas.
Solo este mascarón,
este mascarón de vieja escarlatina,
¡solo este mascarón!

I was on the terrace struggling with the moon.
Swarms of windows riddled with bullets a thigh of night.
The sweet cows of the heavens drank from my eyes.
And the breeze of long oars
struck the cindered windows of Broadway.

The drop of blood sought the light of the star's yolk
to feign a dead apple seed.
The air of the plain, driven by shepherds,
trembled with the fear of a mollusk without its shell.

But it isn't the dead who dance,
I am sure.
The dead have been buried and devour their own hands.
It's the others who dance with the mask and strings.
It's the others, those drunk on silver, cold men,
those who grow in the cross of thighs and hard flames,
those who seek the worm in the landscape of ladders,
those in the bank who drink the tears of dead girls
or who eat in the corners tiny pyramids of dawn.

Don't let the Pope dance!
Don't let him!
Or the King
or the millionaire of blue teeth,
or the dry dancers of the cathedrals,
or builders, or emeralds, or madmen, or sodomites.
Only this mask,
mask of old scarlet cloth,
only this mask!

Que ya las cobras silbarán por los últimos pisos,
que ya las ortigas estremecerán patios y terrazas,
que ya la Bolsa será una pirámide de musgo,
que ya vendrán lianas después de los fusiles
y muy pronto, muy pronto, muy pronto.
¡Ay, Wall Street!

El mascarón. ¡Mirad el mascarón!
¡Cómo escupe veneno de bosque
por la angustia imperfecta de Nueva York!

Diciembre 1929

In time the cobra will hiss in the final floors,
the nettles shake patios and porches,
the Market become a pyramid of moss,
the reeds follow the rifles,
and soon, very soon.
Oh, Wall Street!

The mask, look at the mask!
How it spits the forest's venom
through the imperfect anguish of New York!

December 1929

PAISAJE DE LA MULTITUD QUE VOMITA
(Anochecer de Coney Island)

La mujer gorda venía delante
arrancando las raíces y mojando el pergamino de los tambores;
la mujer gorda
que vuelve del revés los pulpos agonizantes.
La mujer gorda, enemiga de la luna,
corría por las calles y los pisos deshabitados
y dejaba por los rincones pequeñas calaveras de paloma
y levantaba las furias de los banquetes de los siglos últimos
y llamaba al demonio del pan por las colinas del cielo
        barrido
y filtraba un ansia de luz en las circulaciones subterráneas.
Son los cementerios, lo sé, son los cementerios
y el dolor de las cocinas enterradas bajo la arena;
son los muertos, los faisanes y las manzanas de otra
        hora
los que nos empujan en la garganta.

Llegaban los rumores de la selva del vómito
con las mujeres vacías, con niños de cera caliente,
con árboles fermentados y camareros incansables
que sirven platos de sal bajo las arpas de la saliva.
Sin remedio, hijo mío, ¡vomita! No hay remedio.
No es el vómito de los húsares sobre los pechos de la prostituta,
ni el vómito del gato que se tragó una rana por descuido.
Son los muertos que arañan con sus manos de tierra
las puertas de pedernal donde se pudren nublos y postres.

La mujer gorda venía delante
con las gentes de los barcos y de las tabernas y de los jardines.
El vómito agitaba delicadamente sus tambores
entre algunas niñas de sangre
que pedían protección a la luna.

LANDSCAPE OF THE VOMITING CROWD
(Twilight at Coney Island)

The fat woman came in front
tearing up roots and wetting the skins of drums;
the fat woman
who turns agonizing octopi inside out.
The fat woman, enemy of the moon,
ran through the streets and empty apartments
and left in the corners small pigeon skulls
and raised the furies of last century's banquets
and called on the demon of bread through the hills of the
    barren sky
and filtered a hunger for light in the underground traffic.
These are the graveyards, I know it, these are the graveyards
and the sadness of kitchens buried under sand;
these are the dead, the pheasants and the apples of another
    hour
pushing through our throats.

The rumbling came from the jungle of vomit
with empty women, with children of hot wax,
with fermented trees and tireless waiters
who serve dishes of salt under harps of saliva.
No cure, my son, so vomit! There is no cure.
It isn't the vomit of the horsemen on the breasts of whores
or the vomit of the cat that swallows a frog by mistake.
These are the dead who claw with earthen hands
the doors of flint where clouds and sweets are rotting.

The fat woman came in front
with the people from the ships, the bars, and gardens.
The vomit delicately beat its drums
among some girls of blood
who sought protection of the moon.

Federico García Lorca / 49

¡Ay de mí! ¡Ay de mí! ¡Ay de mí!
Esta mirada mía fue mía, pero ya no es mía,
esta mirada que tiembla desnuda por el alcohol
y despide barcos increíbles
por las anémonas de los muelles.
Me defiendo con esta mirada
que mana de las ondas por donde el alba no se atreve,
yo, poeta sin brazos, perdido
entre la multitud que vomita,
sin caballo efusivo que corte
los espesos musgos de mis sienes.

Pero la mujer gorda seguía delante
y la gente buscaba las farmacias
donde el amargo trópico se fija.
Solo cuando izaron la bandera y llegaron los primeros canes
la ciudad entera se agolpó en las barandillas del embarcadero.

New York, 29 de diciembre de 1929.

¡Ay de mí! ¡Ay de mí!
This look of mine was mine, but then was mine no more,
this look that trembles naked in alcohol
and sees off incredible ships
through the anemones of the docks.
I defend myself with this look
that pours from the waves where dawn dares not go.
I, armless poet, lost
in the vomiting crowd
without an effusive horse to cut
the dense moss from my temples.

But the fat woman continued in front
and the people looked for pharmacies
where the bitter tropic is.
Only when they raised the flag and the first dogs arrived
the entire city rushed to the boardwalk's railings.

New York, December 29, 1929

PAISAJE DE LA MULTITUD QUE ORINA
(Nocturno de Battery Place)

Se quedaron solos:
aguardaban la velocidad de las últimas bicicletas.
Se quedaron solas:
esperaban la muerte de un niño en el velero japonés.
Se quedaron solos y solas,
soñando con los picos abiertos de los pájaros agonizantes,
con el agudo quitasol que pincha
al sapo recién aplastado,
bajo un silencio con mil orejas
y diminutas bocas de agua
en los desfiladeros que resisten
el ataque violento de la luna.
Lloraba el niño del velero y se quebraban los corazones
angustiados por el testigo y la vigilia de todas las cosas
y porque todavía en el suelo celeste de negras huellas
gritaban nombres oscuros, salivas y radios de níquel.
No importa que el niño calle cuando le clavan el último
        alfiler,
ni importa la derrota de la brisa en la corola del algodón,
porque hay un mundo de la muerte con marineros
        definitivos
que se asomarán a los arcos y os helarán por detrás de los
        árboles.
Es inútil buscar el recodo
donde la noche olvida su viaje
y acechar un silencio que no tenga
trajes rotos y cáscaras y llanto,
porque tan solo el diminuto banquete de la araña
basta para romper el equilibrio de todo el cielo.
No hay remedio para el gemido del velero japonés,
ni para estas gentes ocultas que tropiezan con las esquinas.

LANDSCAPE OF THE URINATING CROWD
(Nocturne of Battery Place)

The men remained alone:
they awaited the speed of the last bicycles.
The women remained alone:
they awaited the death of a boy in a Japanese sailboat.
The men alone, the women alone,
dreaming of the open beaks of dying birds
and the sharp umbrella that pricks
the newly flattened frog,
under a silence of a thousand ears
and tiny mouths of water
in the canyons that resist
the violent attack of the moon.
The boy of the sailboat wept and hearts broke
anguished by the witness and vigil of all things.
In the celestial ground of black footprints the hearts
still were screaming the dark names, saliva, and radios of
    nickel.
It doesn't matter that the boy is quiet when they pierce him
    with the final pin,
it doesn't matter that the breeze is defeated in the corolla of
    cotton,
because there is a world of death with definitive sailors
who will appear under arches and freeze you behind the trees.
It's useless to look for the bend
where the night forgets its voyage,
useless to stalk a silence
with no broken dresses and rinds and tears,
because the tiny banquet of the spider
is enough to break the equilibrium of the whole sky.
There's no remedy for the moan of the Japanese sailboat,
or for these hidden people who stumble on corners.

El campo se muerde la cola para unir las raíces en un punto
y el ovillo busca por la grama su ansia de longitud insatisfecha.
¡La luna! Los policías. ¡Las sirenas de los transatlánticos!
Fachada de orín, de humo; anémonas, guantes de goma.
Todo está roto por la noche,
abierta de piernas sobre las terrazas.
Todo está roto por los tibios caños
de una terrible fuente silenciosa.
¡Oh gentes! ¡Oh mujercillas! ¡Oh soldados!
Será preciso viajar por los ojos de los idiotas,
campos libres donde silban las mansas cobras de alambradas,
paisajes llenos de sepulcros que producen fresquísimas
     manzanas,
para que venga la luz desmedida
que temen los ricos detrás de sus lupas,
el olor de un solo cuerpo con la doble vertiente de lis y rata
y para que se quemen estas gentes que pueden orinar alrededor
     de un gemido
o en los cristales donde se comprenden las olas nunca
     repetidas.

The countryside bites its tail to join its roots in a point
and the tangle seeks in the grass its anguish of frustrated
    longitude.
The moon! The police. The siren calls of transatlantic liners!
Façade of urine, of smoke, anemones, rubber gloves.
All is broken in the night,
its legs spread wide open over the terraces.
All is broken in the warm pipes
of a terrible, silent fountain.
People! Wounded little women! Soldiers!
You'll have to travel into the eyes of idiots,
open fields where the tamed cobras of barbed wire hiss,
landscapes full of graves that yield the freshest apples,
so that behind the magnifying glass
comes the blinding light that rich men fear,
the smell of a single body with the double slope of iris and rat.
They burn, these people who can piss around a moan
or on windows where we understand the never-repeated waves.

ASESINATO
(Dos voces de madrugada en Riverside Drive)

¿Cómo fue?
—Una grieta en la mejilla.
¡Eso es todo!
Una uña que aprieta el tallo.
Un alfiler que bucea
hasta encontrar las raicillas del grito.
Y el mar deja de moverse.
—*¿Cómo, cómo fue?*
—Así.
—*¡Déjame! ¿De esa manera?*
—Sí.
El corazón salió solo.
—*¡Ay, ay de mí!*

MURDER
(Two voices at dawn on Riverside Drive)

How did it happen?
—A gash on the cheek.
That's all!
A fingernail that squeezes the stem.
A needle that dives
until it finds the small roots of a cry.
And the sea stops moving.
—How, how did it happen?
—Like that.
—Let me go! Like that?
—Yes.
The heart went out alone.
—*¡Ay de mí!*

NAVIDAD EN EL HUDSON

¡Esa esponja gris!
Ese marinero recién degollado.
Ese río grande.
Esa brisa de límites oscuros.
Ese filo, amor, ese filo.
Estaban los cuatro marineros luchando con el mundo,
con el mundo de aristas que ven todos los ojos,
con el mundo que no se puede recorrer sin caballos.
Estaban uno, cien, mil marineros,
luchando con el mundo de las agudas velocidades,
sin enterarse de que el mundo
estaba solo por el cielo.

El mundo solo por el cielo solo.
Son las colinas de martillos y el triunfo de la hierba espesa.
Son los vivísimos hormigueros y las monedas en el fango.
El mundo solo por el cielo solo
y el aire a la salida de todas las aldeas.

Cantaba la lombriz el terror de la rueda
y el marinero degollado
cantaba al oso de agua que lo había de estrechar;
y todos cantaban aleluya,
aleluya. Cielo desierto.
Es lo mismo, ¡lo mismo!, aleluya.

He pasado toda la noche en los andamios de los arrabales
dejándome la sangre por la escayola de los proyectos,
ayudando a los marineros a recoger las velas desgarradas.
Y estoy con las manos vacías en el rumor de la des-
    embocadura.

CHRISTMAS ON THE HUDSON

That gray sponge!
That sailor with his throat just slashed.
That great river.
That breeze of dark limits.
That edge, love, that edge.
Four sailors were struggling with the world,
with the world of chaff that all eyes see,
the world you can't cross without horses.
One, a hundred, a thousand sailors
were struggling with the world of high velocities,
without realizing the world
was alone in the sky.

The world alone in the lonely sky.
These are the hills of hammers and the triumph of thick grass.
These are the swarming anthills and coins in mud.
The world alone in the lonely sky
and the air in the outskirts of all the towns.

The worm sang the terror of the wheel
and the slashed sailor
sang to the bear of water that would embrace his body
and all sang alleluia,
alleluia. Deserted sky.
It's the same, the same! Alleluia.

I've spent the whole night on the scaffolding of the city's
        outskirts
leaving my blood on the plaster of the projects,
helping the sailors rein in the torn sails.
And I am empty-handed in the murmur of the river's
        mouth.

No importa que cada minuto
un niño nuevo agite sus ramitos de venas,
ni que el parto de la víbora, desatado bajo las ramas,
calme la sed de sangre de los que miran el desnudo.
Lo que importa es esto: hueco. Mundo solo. Desembocadura.
Alba no. Fábula inerte.
Solo esto: desembocadura.
¡Oh esponja mía gris!
¡Oh cuello mío recién degollado!
¡Oh río grande mío!
¡Oh brisa mía de límites que no son míos!
¡Oh filo de mi amor, oh hiriente filo!

New York, 27 de diciembre de 1929

It doesn't matter that each minute
a new child shakes his small bunches of veins
or that the newborn viper, let loose under the branches,
calms the blood-thirst of those who look at the nude.
What matters is this: void. The world alone. The river's mouth.
Not dawn. Inert fable.
Only this: the river's mouth.
O my gray sponge!
O my throat slashed!
O my great river!
O my breeze of limits that aren't mine!
O edge of my love, O wounding edge!

New York, December 27, 1929

CIUDAD SIN SUEÑO
(Nocturno del Brooklyn Bridge)

No duerme nadie por el cielo. Nadie, nadie.
No duerme nadie.
Las criaturas de la luna huelen y rondan sus cabañas.
Vendrán las iguanas vivas a morder a los hombres que no
     sueñan
y el que huye con el corazón roto encontrará por las esquinas
al increíble cocodrilo quieto bajo la tierna protesta de los astros.

No duerme nadie por el mundo. Nadie, nadie.
No duerme nadie.
Hay un muerto en el cementerio más lejano
que se queja tres años
porque tiene un paisaje seco en la rodilla;
y el niño que enterraron esta mañana lloraba tanto
que hubo necesidad de llamar a los perros para que callase.

No es sueño la vida. ¡Alerta! ¡Alerta! ¡Alerta!
Nos caemos por las escaleras para comer la tierra húmeda
o subimos al filo de la nieve con el coro de las dalias muertas.
Pero no hay olvido, ni sueño:
carne viva. Los besos atan las bocas
en una maraña de venas recientes
y al que le duele su dolor le dolerá sin descanso
y el que teme la muerte la llevará sobre sus hombros.

Un día
los caballos vivirán en las tabernas
y las hormigas furiosas
atacarán los cielos amarillos que se refugian en los ojos de las
     vacas.

CITY WITHOUT SLEEP
(Nocturne of the Brooklyn Bridge)

No one sleeps in the sky. No one.
No one sleeps.
The creatures of the moon smell and circle their cabins.
Live iguanas will come to bite the men who don't dream
and he who flees with broken heart will find on the corners
the still, incredible crocodile under the tender protest of the
      stars.

No one sleeps in the world. No one.
No one sleeps.
There is a dead man in the farthest cemetery
who for three years complains
of the dry landscape on his knee;
and the boy they buried this morning wept so much
they had to call the dogs to quiet him down.

Life is not a dream. Look!
We fall down the stairs to eat damp earth
or we ascend to the edge of snow with a chorus of dead dahlias.
But there's no forgetting, no sleep:
living flesh. Kisses bind the lips
in a tangle of recent veins
and those who suffer, suffer without rest
and those who fear death will carry it on their shoulders.

One day
horses will live in the taverns
and furious ants
will attack the yellow skies that take refuge in the eyes of cows.

Otro día
veremos la resurrección de las mariposas disecadas
y aun andando por un paisaje de esponjas grises y barcos mudos
veremos brillar nuestro anillo y manar rosas de nuestra lengua.
¡Alerta! ¡Alerta! ¡Alerta!
A los que guardan todavía huellas de zarpa y aguacero,
a aquel muchacho que llora porque no sabe la invención del
        puente
o a aquel muerto que ya no tiene más que la cabeza y un
        zapato,
hay que llevarlos al muro donde iguanas y sierpes esperan,
donde espera la dentadura del oso,
donde espera la mano momificada del niño
y la piel del camello se eriza con un violento escalofrío azul.

No duerme nadie por el cielo. Nadie, nadie.
No duerme nadie.
Pero si alguien cierra los ojos,
¡azotadlo, hijos míos, azotadlo!
Haya un panorama de ojos abiertos
y amargas llagas encendidas.
No duerme nadie por el mundo. Nadie, nadie.

Ya lo he dicho.
No duerme nadie.
Pero si alguien tiene por la noche exceso de musgo en las
        sienes,
abrid los escotillones para que vea bajo la luna
las copas falsas, el veneno y la calavera de los teatros.

Some other day
we'll see the resurrection of mounted butterflies
and even as we wander through a landscape of gray sponges
        and mute ships
we'll see our ring glow and roses pour forth from our tongue.
Look!
Those who still bear traces of claw and squall,
that boy who cries because he knows nothing of the invention
        of the bridge
or that dead man who has only his head and one shoe,
they must be taken to the wall where iguanas and serpents are
        waiting,
where the bear's teeth are waiting,
where a child's mummified hand is waiting,
and the hair of the camel bristles with a violent blue chill.

No one sleeps in the sky. No one.
No one sleeps.
But if someone closes his eyes,
beat him, my children, beat him!
Even if there's a panorama of open eyes
and bitter incandescent sores.
No one sleeps in the world. No one.

I've already said it.
No one sleeps.
But if at night someone has an excess of moss on his temples,
then open the trap doors so the moon lets him see
the false cups, the poison, and the skull of the theaters.

PANORAMA CIEGO DE NUEVA YORK

Si no son los pájaros
cubiertos de ceniza,
si no son los gemidos que golpean las ventanas de la boda,
serán las delicadas criaturas del aire
que manan la sangre nueva por la oscuridad inextinguible.
Pero no, no son los pájaros,
porque los pájaros están a punto de ser bueyes;
pueden ser rocas blancas con la ayuda de la luna
y son siempre muchachos heridos
antes de que los jueces levanten la tela.

Todos comprenden el dolor que se relaciona con la muerte,
pero el verdadero dolor no está presente en el espíritu.
No está en el aire ni en nuestra vida,
ni en estas terrazas llenas de humo.
El verdadero dolor que mantiene despiertas las cosas
es una pequeña quemadura infinita
en los ojos inocentes de los otros sistemas.

Un traje abandonado pesa tanto en los hombros
que muchas veces el cielo los agrupa en ásperas manadas.
Y las que mueren de parto saben en la última hora
que todo rumor será piedra y toda huella latido.
Nosotros ignoramos que el pensamiento tiene arrabales
donde el filósofo es devorado por los chinos y las orugas.
Y algunos niños idiotas han encontrado por las cocinas
pequeñas golondrinas con muletas
que sabían pronunciar la palabra amor.

No, no son los pájaros.
No es un pájaro el que expresa la turbia fiebre de laguna,
ni el ansia de asesinato que nos oprime cada momento,
ni el metálico rumor de suicidio que nos anima cada madrugada.

BLIND PANORAMA OF NEW YORK

If it isn't the birds
covered with ashes,
if it isn't the cries beating on the windows of the wedding,
it must be the delicate creatures of air
that pour out new blood in the unending night.
But no, it isn't the birds
because the birds are ready to be oxen;
they can be white rocks with the aid of the moon
and are always wounded youths before
the judges raise the sheet.

Everyone understands the grief that comes with death
but true grief is not present in the spirit.
It isn't in the air or in our lives
or in these terraces full of smoke.
True grief that keeps things awake
is a small infinite burn
in the innocent eyes of other systems.

An abandoned suit weighs so much on the shoulders
that many times the sky gathers them in rugged herds.
And the women who die in childbirth know in their final hour
that every rumor will be stone and every footprint pulse.
We ignore that thought has outlying boroughs
where the philosopher is devoured by Chinamen and caterpillars.
And some idiot children have found in the kitchen
small swallows on crutches
that knew how to say the word love.

No, it isn't the birds.
It isn't a bird that expresses the clouded pond-like fever
or the longing for murder that oppresses us each minute
or the metallic suicidal rumor that gives breath to each dawn.

Federico García Lorca / 67

Es una cápsula de aire donde nos duele todo el mundo,
es un pequeño espacio vivo al loco unisón de la luz,
es una escala indefinible donde las nubes y rosas olvidan
el griterío chino que bulle por el desembarcadero de la sangre.
Yo muchas veces me he perdido
para buscar la quemadura que mantiene despiertas las cosas
y solo he encontrado marineros echados sobre las barandillas
y pequeñas criaturas del cielo enterradas bajo la nieve.
Pero el verdadero dolor estaba en otras plazas
donde los peces cristalizados agonizaban dentro de los troncos;
plazas del cielo extraño para las antiguas estatuas ilesas
y para la tierna intimidad de los volcanes.

No hay dolor en la voz. Solo existen los dientes,
pero dientes que callarán aislados por el raso negro.
No hay dolor en la voz. Aquí solo existe la tierra.
La tierra con sus puertas de siempre
que llevan al rubor de los frutos.

It's a capsule of air where the whole world hurts us,
it's a small living space to the crazy unison of light,
it's an undefinable scale where clouds and roses forget
the Chinese clamor that bustles on the docks of blood.
Many times I've lost myself
in order to search for the burn that keeps things awake
and I've only found sailors leaning over the railing
and small creatures of the sky buried under snow.
But real grief was in other plazas
where crystallized fish agonized inside the tree trunks;
plazas of a strange sky for the ancient untouched statues
and for the tender intimacy of volcanoes.

There's no grief in my voice. Only my teeth exist,
teeth that go silent in the isolation of black satin.
There's no grief in my voice. Here only the earth exists,
the earth with the doors of forever
that lead to the shame of fruit.

NACIMIENTO DE CRISTO

Un pastor pide teta por la nieve que ondula
blancos perros tendidos entre linternas sordas.
El Cristito de barro se ha partido los dedos
en los filos eternos de la madera rota.

¡Ya vienen las hormigas y los pies ateridos!
Dos hilillos de sangre quiebran el cielo duro.
Los vientres del demonio resuenan por los valles
golpes y resonancias de carne de molusco.

Lobos y sapos cantan en las hogueras verdes
coronadas por vivos hormigueros del alba.
La luna tiene un sueño de grandes abanicos
y el toro sueña un toro de agujeros y de agua.

El niño llora y mira con un tres en la frente.
San José ve en el heno tres espinas de bronce.
Los pañales exhalan un rumor de desierto
con cítaras sin cuerdas y degolladas voces.

La nieve de Manhattan empuja los anuncios
y lleva gracia pura por las falsas ojivas.
Sacerdotes idiotas y querubes de pluma
van detrás de Lutero por las altas esquinas.

BIRTH OF CHRIST

A shepherd asks for a teat in the snow
that waves white dogs lying among deaf lamps.
The small clay Christ has broken its fingers
on the eternal edges of split wood.

Now come the ants and the stiff frozen feet!
Two small streams of blood break through the hard sky.
Wombs of the devil sound through the valleys,
blows and resonances of mollusk meat.

Wolves and toads sing in the green bonfires
that are crowned by swarming anthills of dawn.
The moon has a dream of giant fans and
the bull dreams a bull of holes and water.

With a three on his brow, the boy cries, stares.
In the hay Saint Joseph sees three bronze thorns.
From the newborn's clothes, a desert murmur
comes with stringless zithers and slashed voices.

Snow in Manhattan pushes the billboards
and brings pure grace to false pointed arches.
Idiot priests and cherubs of feather
follow Luther past all the high corners.

LA AURORA

La aurora de Nueva York tiene
cuatro columnas de cieno
y un huracán de negras palomas
que chapotean las aguas podridas.

La aurora de Nueva York gime
por las inmensas escaleras
buscando entre las aristas
nardos de angustia dibujada.

La aurora llega y nadie la recibe en su boca
porque allí no hay mañana ni esperanza posible.
A veces las monedas en enjambres furiosos
taladran y devoran abandonados niños.

Los primeros que salen comprenden con sus huesos
que no habrá paraíso ni amores deshojados;
saben que van al cieno de números y leyes,
a los juegos sin arte, a sudores sin fruto.

La luz es sepultada por cadenas y ruidos
en impúdico reto de ciencia sin raíces.
Por los barrios hay gentes que vacilan insomnes
como recién salidas de un naufragio de sangre.

DAWN

Dawn in New York
has four columns of filth
and a hurricane of black doves
splashing in putrid waters.

Dawn in New York whimpers
down the huge stairs
seeking in the chaff
flowers of sketched anguish.

Dawn comes and no one receives it in his mouth
because there is no tomorrow or possibility of hope.
Sometimes furious swarms of coins
drill and devour the abandoned children.

The first to leave understand in their bones
there'll be no paradise or leafless loves;
they know they go to the filth of numbers and laws,
to artless games, to fruitless sweat.

The light is buried by noises and chains
in the obscene challenge of rootless science.
In the neighborhoods are people who wander unsleeping
like survivors of a shipwreck of blood.

IV
Poemas del lago Eden Mills

A Eduardo Ugarte

IV
Poems of Lake Eden Mills

To Eduardo Ugarte

POEMA DOBLE DEL LAGO EDEN

Nuestro ganado pace, el viento espira.
— Garcilaso

Era mi voz antigua
ignorante de los densos jugos amargos.
La adivino lamiendo mis pies
bajo los frágiles helechos mojados.

¡Ay voz antigua de mi amor,
ay voz de mi verdad,
ay voz de mi abierto costado,
cuando todas las rosas manaban de mi lengua
y el césped no conocía la impasible dentadura del caballo!

Estás aquí bebiendo mi sangre,
bebiendo mi humor de niño pesado,
mientras mis ojos se quiebran en el viento
con el aluminio y las voces de los borrachos.

Déjame pasar la puerta
donde Eva come hormigas
y Adán fecunda peces deslumbrados.
Déjame pasar, hombrecillo de los cuernos,
al bosque de los desperezos
y los alegrísimos saltos.

Yo sé el uso más secreto
que tiene un viejo alfiler oxidado
y sé del horror de unos ojos despiertos
sobre la superficie concreta del plato.

DOUBLE POEM OF LAKE EDEN

Our cattle graze, the wind exhales.
            —Garcilaso

It was my old voice,
ignorant of the dense, bitter juices.
I imagine her licking my feet
under the wet, fragile ferns.

Old voice of my love,
voice of my truth,
voice of my open side,
when all the roses flowed from my tongue
and the lawn didn't know the horse's impassive teeth!

You're here drinking my blood,
drinking my pissy boy humor,
while my eyes shatter in the wind
with the aluminum and the voice of drunks.

Let me pass the door
where Eve eats ants
and Adam fertilizes dazzled fish.
Let me pass, little man with horns,
to the forest of waking
and joyful leaps.

I know the most secret use
for an old, rusted pin
and I know the horror of wide-awake eyes
on the concrete surface of the dish.

Pero no quiero mundo ni sueño, voz divina,
quiero mi libertad, mi amor humano
en el rincón más oscuro de la brisa que nadie quiera.
¡Mi amor humano!

Esos perros marinos se persiguen
y el viento acecha troncos descuidados.
¡Oh voz antigua, quema con tu lengua
esta voz de hojalata y de talco!

Quiero llorar porque me da la gana
como lloran los niños del último banco,
porque yo no soy un hombre, ni un poeta, ni una hoja,
pero sí un pulso herido que sonda las cosas del otro lado.

Quiero llorar diciendo mi nombre,
rosa, niño y abeto a la orilla de este lago,
para decir mi verdad de hombre de sangre
matando en mí la burla y la sugestión del vocablo.

No, no, yo no pregunto, yo deseo,
voz mía libertada que me lames las manos.
En el laberinto de biombos es mi desnudo el que recibe
la luna de castigo y el reloj encenizado.

Así hablaba yo.
Así hablaba yo cuando Saturno detuvo los trenes
y la bruma y el Sueño y la Muerte me estaban buscando.
Me estaban buscando
allí donde mugen las vacas que tienen patitas de paje
y allí donde flota mi cuerpo entre los equilibrios contrarios.

But I don't want world or dream, divine voice,
I want my freedom, my human love
in the darkest corner of the breeze that no one wants.
My human love!

Those sea dogs chase each other
and the wind stalks careless tree trunks.
Old voice, burn with your tongue
this voice of tin and talc!

I want to cry because I feel like it
as the boys in the back row cry,
because I am not a man or a poet or a leaf
but a wounded pulse that probes the things of the other side.

I want to cry saying my name,
rose, boy, and fir on the shore of this lake,
to say my truth of a man of blood
killing in me the deceit and suggestion of words.

No, I don't question, I desire,
freed voice of mine that licks my hands.
In the labyrinth of folding screens my nakedness receives
the moon of punishment and the ashen clock.

This is the way I spoke.
This is the way I spoke when Saturn stopped the trains
and the fog and Sleep and Death went looking for me.
They went looking for me
there where the cows low with their bellhop feet
and my body floats balanced between opposites.

CIELO VIVO

Yo no podré quejarme
si no encontré lo que buscaba.
Cerca de las piedras sin jugo y los insectos vacíos
no veré el duelo del sol con las criaturas en carne viva.

Pero me iré al primer paisaje
de choques, líquidos y rumores
que trasmina a niño recién nacido
y donde toda superficie es evitada,
para entender que lo que busco tendrá su blanco de alegría
cuando yo vuele mezclado con el amor y las arenas.

Allí no llega la escarcha de los ojos apagados
ni el mugido del árbol asesinado por la oruga.
Allí todas las formas guardan entrelazadas
una sola expresión frenética de avance.

No puedes avanzar por los enjambres de corolas
porque el aire disuelve tus dientes de azúcar,
ni puedes acariciar la fugaz hoja del helecho
sin sentir el asombro definitivo del marfil.

Allí bajo las raíces y en la médula del aire,
se comprende la verdad de las cosas equivocadas,
el nadador de níquel que acecha la onda más fina
y el rebaño de vacas nocturnas con rojas patitas de mujer.

Yo no podré quejarme
si no encontré lo que buscaba;
pero me iré al primer paisaje de humedades y latidos
para entender que lo que busco tendrá su blanco de alegría
cuando yo vuele mezclado con el amor y las arenas.

LIVING SKY

I won't complain
if I don't find what I was looking for.
Near the dried stones and the empty insects
I won't see the sun dueling with creatures of living flesh.

But I'll go to the first landscape
of shocks, liquids and murmurs
that smell of a newborn child,
and there where surface is avoided
to understand what I seek must have a target of joy
as I fly in the midst of love and sand.

The frost of spent eyes doesn't reach there
or the bellow of a tree murdered by the worm.
All forms are interlaced there
with the same frenetic expression of progress.

You can't advance through the swarms of corollas
because the air dissolves your sugar teeth
or caress the fleeting fern leaf
without feeling the ultimate ivory surprise.

There, under the roots, in the medulla of air,
we understand the truth of mistaken things,
the chrome swimmer who spies the finest wave
and the flock of nocturnal cattle with the tiny red feet of a woman.

I won't complain
if I don't find what I was looking for,
but I'll go to the first landscape of dampness and pulse
to understand what I seek must have a target of joy
as I fly in the midst of love and sand.

Federico García Lorca / 81

Vuelo fresco de siempre sobre lechos vacíos,
sobre grupos de brisas y barcos encallados.
Tropiezo vacilante por la dura eternidad fija
y amor al fin sin alba. Amor. ¡Amor visible!

Eden Mills, Vermont, 24 agosto 1929

I fly in cool air over empty beds,
over collected breezes and ships run aground.
I stumble, waver, through hard, fixed eternity
and a love at last without dawn. Love. Visible love!

Eden Mills, Vermont
August 24, 1929

V
En la cabaña del Farmer
(Campo de Newburg)

A Concha Méndez y Manuel Altolaguirre

V
In the Farmer's Cabin
(Newburgh Countryside)

To Concha Méndez and Manuel Altolaguirre

EL NIÑO STANTON

Do you like me?
—Yes, and you?
—Yes, yes.

Cuando me quedo solo
me quedan todavía tus diez años,
los tres caballos ciegos,
tus quince rostros con el rostro de la pedrada
y las fiebres pequeñas heladas sobre las hojas del maíz.
Stanton, hijo mío, Stanton.
A las doce de la noche el cáncer salía por los pasillos
y hablaba con los caracoles vacíos de los documentos,
el vivísimo cáncer lleno de nubes y termómetros
con su casto afán de manzana para que lo piquen los
      ruiseñores.
En la casa donde hay un cáncer
se quiebran las blancas paredes en el delirio de la astronomía
y por los establos más pequeños y en las cruces de los bosques
brilla por muchos años el fulgor de la quemadura.
Mi dolor sangraba por las tardes
cuando tus ojos eran dos muros,
cuando tus manos eran dos países
y mi cuerpo rumor de hierba.
Mi agonía buscaba su traje,
polvorienta, mordida por los perros,
y tú la acompañaste sin temblar
hasta la puerta del agua oscura.
¡Oh mi Stanton, idiota y bello entre los pequeños animalitos,
con tu madre fracturada por los herreros de las aldeas,
con un hermano bajo los arcos,

THE BOY STANTON

Do you like me?
—Yes, and you?
—Yes, yes.

When I am alone
your ten years still are with me,
the three blind horses,
your fifteen faces with the face of flung stone
and the small fevers frozen on leaves of corn.
Stanton, my son, Stanton.
At midnight, the cancer came through the hallways
and talked with the empty seashells of documents,
the most living cancer full of clouds and thermometers
with the chaste eagerness of an apple the nightingales peck.
In the house where there's a cancer
the white walls break in the delirium of astronomy
and in the smallest stables and the crossroads of the forest
for many years the burning splendor glows.
My sorrow bloodied the afternoons
when your eyes were two walls,
when your hands were two countries,
and my body a murmur of grass.
My agony sought its clothing,
dusty, dog-bitten,
and you accompanied it without trembling
to the door of dark water.
O, my Stanton, idiotic and beautiful among the smallest
	animals,
with your mother broken by the town's blacksmiths,
with a brother under the arches,

otro comido por los hormigueros,
y el cáncer sin alambradas latiendo por las habitaciones!
Hay nodrizas que dan a los niños
ríos de musgo y amargura de pie
y algunas negras suben a los pisos para repartir filtro
      de rata.
Porque es verdad que la gente
quiere echar las palomas a las alcantarillas
y yo sé lo que esperan los que por la calle
nos oprimen de pronto las yemas de los dedos.

Tu ignorancia es un monte de leones, Stanton.
El día que el cáncer te dio una paliza
y te escupió en el dormitorio donde murieron los huéspedes
      en la epidemia
y abrió su quebrada rosa de vidrios secos y manos blandas
para salpicar de lodo las pupilas de los que navegan,
tú buscaste en la hierba mi agonía,
mi agonía con flores de terror,
mientras que el agrio cáncer mudo que quiere acostarse contigo
pulverizaba rojos paisajes por las sábanas de amargura,
y ponía sobre los ataúdes
helados arbolitos de ácido bórico.
Stanton, vete al bosque con tus arpas judías,
vete para aprender celestiales palabras
que duermen en los troncos, en nubes, en tortugas,
en los perros dormidos, en el plomo, en el viento,
en lirios que no duermen, en aguas que no copian,
para que aprendas, hijo, lo que tu pueblo olvida.

Cuando empiece el tumulto de la guerra
dejaré un pedazo de queso para tu perro en la oficina.
Tus diez años serán las hojas
que vuelan en los trajes de los muertos,

another eaten on the anthills,
and the unwired cancer beating through the bedrooms!
There are wet-nurses who give the children
rivers of moss and bitterness of foot
and some black women who go up to the apartments to put out
    rat potion.
Because it's true that the people
want to throw the doves down the sewers
and I know what they wait for, those on the street
who suddenly press the tips of our fingers.

Your ignorance is a mountain of lions, Stanton.
The day that the cancer gave you a beating
it spit at you in the bedroom where the guests died in the
    epidemic.
It opened its broken rose of dry crystal and soft hands
to splash mud in the pupils of those who sail.
You looked in the grass for my agony,
my agony with flowers of terror,
while the sour, mute cancer that wants to sleep with you
pulverized red landscapes on the bedsheets of bitterness,
and placed on the coffins
small frozen trees of boric acid.
Stanton, go to the forest with your Jew's harp,
go learn the heavenly words
that sleep in the trunks, in clouds, in tortoises,
in sleeping dogs, in lead, in the wind,
in the sleepless lilies, in unrepeating waters,
so that you learn, son, what your people forget.

When the tumult of war begins
I'll leave a piece of cheese for your dog in the office.
Your ten years will be the leaves
that fly in the clothes of the dead,

diez rosas de azufre débil
en el hombro de mi madrugada.
Y yo, Stanton, yo solo, en olvido,
con tus caras marchitas sobre mi boca,
iré penetrando a voces las verdes estatuas de la Malaria.

ten roses of weak sulfur
on the shoulder of my dawn.
And I, Stanton, I alone will go, forgotten,
with your faded faces over my mouth,
loudly piercing the green statues of Malaria.

VACA

A Luis Lacasa

Se tendió la vaca herida.
Árboles y arroyos trepaban por sus cuernos.
Su hocico sangraba en el cielo.

Su hocico de abejas
bajo el bigote lento de la baba.
Un alarido blanco puso en pie la mañana.

Las vacas muertas y las vivas,
rubor de luz o miel de establo,
balaban con los ojos entornados.

Que se enteren las raíces
y aquel niño que afila su navaja
de que ya se pueden comer la vaca.

Arriba palidecen
luces y yugulares.
Cuatro pezuñas tiemblan en el aire.

Que se entere la luna
y esa noche de rocas amarillas:
que ya se fue la vaca de ceniza.

Que ya se fue balando
por el derribo de los cielos yertos
donde meriendan muerte los borrachos.

COW

To Luis Lacasa

The wounded cow lay down.
Trees and streams climbed up its horns.
Its muzzle bled in the sky.

Its muzzle of bees
under the slow mustache of drool.
A white scream brought the morning to its feet.

The dead cows and the living,
flush of light or honey from the stable,
lowed with eyes half-closed.

Let the roots know
and that boy who sharpens his blade
that now they can eat the cow.

Above, lights
and jugulars grow pale.
Four hoofs tremble in midair.

Let the moon know
and that night of yellow rocks:
that the ashen cow's already gone.

That it went lowing
through the rubble of the stiff sky
where the drunks snack on death.

NIÑA AHOGADA EN EL POZO

(Granada y Newburg)

Las estatuas sufren por los ojos con la oscuridad de los ataúdes,
pero sufren mucho más por el agua que no desemboca.
Que no desemboca.

El pueblo corría por las almenas rompiendo las cañas de los
      pescadores.
¡Pronto! ¡Los bordes! ¡De prisa! Y croaban las estrellas
      tiernas.
. . . que no desemboca.

Tranquila en mi recuerdo, astro, círculo, meta,
lloras por las orillas de un ojo de caballo.
. . . que no desemboca.

Pero nadie en lo oscuro podrá darte distancias,
sino afilado límite, porvenir de diamante.
. . . que no desemboca.

Mientras la gente busca silencios de almohada
tú lates para siempre definida en tu anillo.
. . . que no desemboca.

Eterna en los finales de unas ondas que aceptan
combate de raíces y soledad prevista.
. . . que no desemboca.

¡Ya vienen por las rampas! ¡Levántate del agua!
¡Cada punto de luz te dará una cadena!
. . . que no desemboca.

GIRL DROWNED IN THE WELL

(Granada and Newburgh)

The statues suffer with their eyes the darkness of coffins
but suffer even more from the water not flowing to the sea.
Not flowing.

The people ran to the battlements, breaking the fishermen's
     poles.
Hurry! To the edges! Quickly! And from the tender stars,
     croaking, croaking
. . . not flowing.

Tranquil in my memory, star, circle, end,
you weep on the shores of a horse's eye
. . . not flowing.

But no one in the dark could give you distance,
instead a sharp limit, future of diamond
. . . not flowing.

While the people seek the silences of a pillow
you beat forever, defined by your ring
. . . not flowing.

Eternal in final waves that accept
the combat of roots and foreseen solitude
. . . not flowing.

Now they come down the ramps! Rise up from the water!
Each point of light will give you a chain!
. . . not flowing.

Federico García Lorca / 95

Pero el pozo te alarga manecitas de musgo,
insospechada ondina de su casta ignorancia.
. . . que no desemboca.

No, que no desemboca. Agua fija en un punto,
respirando con todos sus violines sin cuerdas
en la escala de las heridas y los edificios deshabitados.

¡Agua que no desemboca!

The well reaches for you with small hands of moss,
a sprite unaware of its chaste ignorance
. . . not flowing.

No, it's not flowing. Water fixed at a point,
breathing with all the string-less violins
on the scale of wounds and abandoned buildings.

Water not flowing to the sea.

VI
Introducción a la muerte

Poemas de la soledad en Vermont

Para Rafael Sánchez Ventura

VI
Introduction to Death

Poems of Solitude in Vermont

For Rafael Sánchez Ventura

MUERTE

A Luís de la Serna

¡Qué esfuerzo!
¡Qué esfuerzo del caballo por ser perro!
¡Qué esfuerzo del perro por ser golondrina!
¡Qué esfuerzo de la abeja por ser caballo!
Y el caballo,
¡qué flecha aguda exprime de la rosa!,
¡qué rosa gris levanta de su belfo!
Y la rosa,
¡qué rebaño de luces y alaridos
ata en el vivo azúcar de su tronco!
Y el azúcar,
¡qué puñalitos sueña en su vigilia!
Y los puñales diminutos,
¡qué luna sin establos, qué desnudos,
piel eterna y rubor, andan buscando!
Y yo, por los aleros,
¡qué serafín de llamas busco y soy!
Pero el arco de yeso,
¡qué grande, qué invisible, qué diminuto!,
sin esfuerzo.

DEATH

For Luis de la Serna

It's hard!
Hard for the horse to be dog!
Hard for the dog to be swallow!
Hard for the swallow to be bee!
Hard for the bee to be horse!
And the horse,
what sharp arrow it squeezes from the rose!
what gray rose rises from its lips!
And the rose,
what flock of lights and howls
bound in the living sugar of its stem!
And the sugar,
what small daggers it dreams in its vigil!
And the diminutive daggers,
what moon without stables, what nudes,
what flushed, eternal skin they seek!
And I, on the eaves,
what seraph of flame I seek and am!
But the plaster arch:
Large. Invisible. Minute.
So effortless!

NOCTURNO DEL HUECO

I.

Para ver que todo se ha ido,
para ver los huecos y los vestidos,
¡dame tu guante de luna,
tu otro guante perdido en la hierba,
amor mío!

Puede el aire arrancar los caracoles
muertos sobre el pulmón del elefante
y soplar los gusanos ateridos
de las yemas de luz o las manzanas.

Los rostros bogan impasibles
bajo el diminuto griterío de las yerbas
y en el rincón está el pechito de la rana
turbio de corazón y mandolina.

En la gran plaza desierta
mugía la bovina cabeza recién cortada
y eran duro cristal definitivo
las formas que buscaban el giro de la sierpe.

Para ver que todo se ha ido
dame tu mudo hueco, ¡amor mío!
Nostalgia de academia y cielo triste.
¡Para ver que todo se ha ido!

Dentro de ti, amor mío, por tu carne,
¡qué silencio de trenes bocaarriba!,
¡cuánto brazo de momia florecido!,
¡qué cielo sin salida, amor, qué cielo!

NOCTURNE OF THE HOLE

I.

To see that everything has gone,
to see the holes and dresses,
give me your moon glove,
your other glove lost in the grass,
my love!

The air can tear the dead snails
off the elephant's lung
and fan the cold, numb worms
from the buds of light or the apples.

The impassive faces row
under the small screams of grass,
and in the corner is the frog's small chest
troubled by heart and mandolin.

In the great deserted plaza
the bovine head, newly severed, bellowed,
and the shapes were hard definitive crystal
searching for the serpent's coil.

To see that everything has gone,
give me your mute hole, my love!
Nostalgia of academy and sad sky.
To see that everything has gone!

Inside you, my love, through your flesh,
is the silence of upturned trains,
the flowered arm of a mummy,
the sky without exit, love, the sky!

Es la piedra en el agua y es la voz en la brisa
bordes de amor que escapan de su tronco sangrante.
Basta tocar el pulso de nuestro amor presente
para que broten flores sobre los otros niños.

Para ver que todo se ha ido.
Para ver los huecos de nubes y ríos.
Dame tus manos de laurel, amor.
¡Para ver que todo se ha ido!

Ruedan los huecos puros, por mí, por ti, en el alba
conservando las huellas de las ramas de sangre
y algún perfil de yeso tranquilo que dibuja
instantáneo dolor de luna apuntillada.

Mira formas concretas que buscan su vacío.
Perros equivocados y manzanas mordidas.
Mira el ansia, la angustia de un triste mundo fósil
que no encuentra el acento de su primer sollozo.

Cuando busco en la cama los rumores del hilo
has venido, amor mío, a cubrir mi tejado.
El hueco de una hormiga puede llenar el aire,
pero tú vas gimiendo sin norte por mis ojos.

No, por mis ojos no, que ahora me enseñas
cuatro ríos ceñidos en tu brazo,
en la dura barraca donde la luna prisionera
devora a un marinero delante de los niños.

Para ver que todo se ha ido
¡amor inexpugnable, amor huido!
No, no me des tu hueco,
¡que ya va por el aire el mío!
¡Ay de ti, ay de mí, de la brisa!
Para ver que todo se ha ido.

It's the stone in water and it's the voice in the breeze,
limits of love that escape their bleeding trunk.
It's enough to touch the pulse of our present love
so that flowers may bloom over other children.

To see that everything has gone.
To see the holes of clouds and rivers.
Give me your laurel hands, love.
To see that everything has gone.

The pure holes roll in me, in you, at dawn,
keeping the traces of the branches of blood
and some profile of quiet plaster drawing
the instant pain of the punctured moon.

Look at concrete shapes seeking their void.
Mistaken dogs and bitten apples.
Look at the longing, the anguish of a sad fossil world
that cannot find the accent of its first sob.

When I look in bed for the murmurs of thread,
you've come, my love, to cover my roof.
An ant hole can fill the air,
but you go moaning without north in my eyes.

No, not in my eyes, now that you show me
four narrow rivers circling your arm,
in the crude shack where the imprisoned moon
devours a sailor in front of the children.

To see that everything has gone,
love unassailable, fleeting love!
No, don't give me your hole
now that mine goes through the air!
Ay de ti, ay de mí, pity the breeze!
To see that everything has gone.

II.

Yo.
Con el hueco blanquísimo de un caballo,
crines de ceniza. Plaza pura y doblada.

Yo.
Mi hueco traspasado con las axilas rotas.
Piel seca de uva neutra y amianto de madrugada.

Toda la luz del mundo cabe dentro de un ojo.
Canta el gallo y su canto dura más que sus alas.

Yo.
Con el hueco blanquísimo de un caballo.
Rodeado de espectadores que tienen hormigas en las palabras.

En el circo del frío sin perfil mutilado.
Por los capiteles rotos de las mejillas desangradas.

Yo.
Mi hueco sin ti, ciudad, sin tus muertos que comen.
Ecuestre por mi vida definitivamente anclada.

Yo.
No hay siglo nuevo ni luz reciente.
Solo un caballo azul y una madrugada.

II.

I.
With the whitest hole of a horse,
ashen manes. Plaza pure and doubled.

I.
My hole run through with broken armpits.
Dry skin of a neuter grape and amianthus of dawn.

All the light of the world fits inside an eye.
The rooster crows and his song lasts longer than his wings.

I.
With the whitest hole of a horse.
Surrounded by spectators with ants in their words.

In the circus of cold without a mutilated profile.
Through the broken capitals of bled cheeks.

I.
My hole without you, city, without your dead who eat.
Equestrian through my fully anchored life.

I.
There's no new century or recent light.
Only a blue horse and dawn.

PAISAJE CON DOS TUMBAS Y UN PERRO ASIRIO

Amigo,
levántate para que oigas aullar
al perro asirio.
Las tres ninfas del cáncer han estado bailando,
hijo mío.
Trajeron unas montañas de lacre rojo
y unas sábanas duras donde estaba el cáncer dormido.
El caballo tenía un ojo en el cuello
y la luna estaba en un cielo tan frío
que tuvo que desgarrarse su monte de Venus
y ahogar en sangre y ceniza los cementerios antiguos.

Amigo,
despierta, que los montes todavía no respiran
y las hierbas de mi corazón están en otro sitio.
No importa que estés lleno de agua de mar.
Yo amé mucho tiempo a un niño
que tenía una plumilla en la lengua
y vivimos cien años dentro de un cuchillo.
Despierta. Calla. Escucha. Incorpórate un poco.

El aullido
es una larga lengua morada que deja
hormigas de espanto y licor de lirios.
Ya viene hacia la roca. ¡No alargues tus raíces!
Se acerca. Gime. No solloces en sueños, amigo.

¡Amigo!
Levántate para que oigas aullar
al perro asirio.

LANDSCAPE WITH TWO TOMBS AND AN ASSYRIAN DOG

Friend,
get up so you can hear
the Assyrian dog howl.
The three nymphs of cancer have been dancing,
my son.
They brought mountains of red sealing wax
and hard sheets where cancer slept.
The horse had an eye on his neck
and the moon was in a sky so cold
she had to tear apart her Venus mound
and drown the ancient cemeteries in blood and ash.

Friend,
wake up, for the mountains still don't breathe
and the grasses of my heart are in another place.
It doesn't matter you are full of seawater.
For a long time I loved a boy
who had a feather on his tongue
and we lived a hundred years inside a knife.
Wake up. Be quiet. Listen. Sit up a little.

The howl
is a long purple tongue that leaves
ants of dread and liquor of lilies.
It's coming to the rock. Don't stretch your roots!
It's coming. It moans. Don't cry in your dreams, friend.

Friend!
Get up so you can hear
the Assyrian dog howl.

RUINA

A Regino Sainz de la Maza

Sin encontrarse,
viajero por su propio torso blanco,
¡así iba el aire!

Pronto se vio que la luna
era una calavera de caballo
y el aire una manzana oscura.

Detrás de la ventana
con látigos y luces se sentía
la lucha de la arena con el agua.

Yo vi llegar las hierbas
y les eché un cordero que balaba
bajo sus dientecillos y lancetas.

Volaba dentro de una gota
la cáscara de pluma y celuloide
de la primera paloma.

Las nubes en manada
se quedaron dormidas contemplando
el duelo de las rocas con el alba.

Vienen las hierbas, hijo.
Ya suenan sus espadas de saliva
por el cielo vacío.

Mi mano, amor. ¡Las hierbas!
Por los cristales rotos de la casa
la sangre desató sus cabelleras.

RUIN

To Regino Sainz de la Maza

Unknown to itself
a traveler through its own white torso,
so went the air!

Soon we saw the moon
was a horse's skull
and the air a dark apple.

Behind the window
with whips and lights, we felt
the struggle of sand with water.

I saw the grasses arrive
and I threw at them a lamb bleating
under their tiny teeth and lancets.

In a drop flew
the feather's shell and the celluloid
of the first dove.

The clouds in a herd
remained asleep, contemplating
the duel of the rocks with dawn.

The grasses come, son.
Already their swords of saliva sound
in the empty sky.

My hand, love. The grasses!
Through the broken windows of the house
blood loosened its long hair.

Federico García Lorca / 111

Tú solo y yo quedamos.
Prepara tu esqueleto para el aire.
Yo solo y tú quedamos.

Prepara tu esqueleto.
Hay que buscar de prisa, amor, de prisa,
nuestro perfil sin sueño.

You alone and I remain.
Prepare your skeleton for the air.
I alone and you remain.

Prepare your skeleton.
One must look quickly, love, quickly,
for our profile without sleep.

LUNA Y PANORAMA DE LOS INSECTOS

(Poema de amor)

> *La luna en el mar riela,*
> *en la lona gime el viento*
> *y alza en blando movimiento*
> *olas de plata y azul.*

> —Espronceda

Mi corazón tendría la forma de un zapato
si cada aldea tuviera una sirena.
Pero la noche es interminable cuando se apoya en los enfermos
y hay barcos que buscan ser mirados para poder hundirse
       tranquilos.

Si el aire sopla blandamente
mi corazón tiene la forma de una niña.
Si el aire se niega a salir de los cañaverales
mi corazón tiene la forma de una milenaria boñiga de toro.

Bogar, bogar, bogar, bogar,
hacia el batallón de puntas desiguales,
hacia un paisaje de acechos pulverizados.
Noche igual de la nieve, de los sistemas suspendidos.
Y la luna.
¡La luna!
Pero no la luna.
La raposa de las tabernas,
el gallo japonés que se comió los ojos,
las hierbas masticadas.

MOON AND PANORAMA OF THE INSECTS

(Love Poem)

> *On the ocean the moon shimmers,*
> *on the canvas the wind moans*
> *and lifts in slow modulation*
> *waves of silver and blue.*

> —Espronceda

My heart would have the shape of a shoe
if every village had a siren.
But night is endless when it leans on the sick
and there are ships that long to be seen before they sink
     in peace.

If the air blows softly
my heart has the shape of a girl.
If the air refuses to leave the cane fields
my heart has the shape of a bull's millennial dung.

To row, to row
toward the battalion of unequal points,
toward a landscape of pulverized stalking.
Night of equal snow, of systems suspended.
And the moon.
The moon!
But not the moon.
The vixen in the taverns,
the Japanese rooster that ate its eyes,
the masticated grass.

No nos salvan las solitarias en los vidrios,
ni los herbolarios donde el metafísico
encuentra las otras vertientes del cielo.
Son mentira las formas. Solo existe
el círculo de bocas del oxígeno.
Y la luna.
Pero no la luna.
Los insectos,
los muertos diminutos por las riberas,
dolor en longitud,
yodo en un punto,
las muchedumbres en el alfiler,
el desnudo que amasa la sangre de todos,
y mi amor que no es un caballo ni una quemadura,
criatura de pecho devorado.
¡Mi amor!

Ya cantan, gritan, gimen: Rostro. ¡Tu rostro! Rostro.
Las manzanas son unas,
las dalias son idénticas,
la luz tiene un sabor de metal acabado
y el campo de todo un lustro cabrá en la mejilla de la moneda.
Pero tu rostro cubre los cielos del banquete.
¡Ya cantan!, ¡gritan!, ¡gimen!,
¡cubren!, ¡trepan!, ¡espantan!

Es necesario caminar, ¡de prisa!, por las ondas, por las ramas,
por las calles deshabitadas de la edad media que bajan al río,
por las tiendas de las pieles donde suena un cuerno de vaca
        herida,
por las escalas, ¡sin miedo!, por las escalas.
Hay un hombre descolorido que se está bañando en el mar;
es tan tierno que los reflectores le comieron jugando el
        corazón.

The tapeworms under glass cannot save us
or the herb store where the metaphysician
finds the other slopes of the sky.
Shapes are lies. Only the circle
of oxygen mouths exists.
And the moon.
But not the moon.
Insects,
the tiny dead along the shore,
sorrow in longitude,
iodine on the point,
multitudes on a pin,
the nude that mixes the blood of all,
and my love that is neither a horse nor a burn
but a creature with its chest devoured.
My love!

Now they sing, scream, moan: Face. Your face! Face.
The apples are one,
the dahlias are identical,
the light has a flavor of finished metal,
and the whole of five years will fit on the cheek of a coin.
But your face covers the skies over the banquet.
Already they sing! Scream! Moan!
Cover! Climb! Frighten!

It's necessary to walk, but quickly through waves, up branches,
down the empty streets of the Middle Ages that descend to the
        river,
past the leather shops and the sound of a wounded cow's horn,
up the ladders, unafraid, up the ladders.
There's a discolored man bathing in the sea,
so tender that searchlights ate his heart in
        play.

Y en el Perú viven mil mujeres, ¡oh insectos!, que noche
    y día
hacen nocturnos y desfiles entrecruzando sus propias venas.

Un diminuto guante corrosivo me detiene. ¡Basta!
En mi pañuelo he sentido el tris
de la primera vena que se rompe.
Cuida tus pies, amor mío, ¡tus manos!,
ya que yo tengo que entregar mi rostro,
mi rostro, ¡mi rostro!, ¡ay, mi comido rostro!

Este fuego casto para mi deseo,
esta confusión por anhelo de equilibrio,
este inocente dolor de pólvora en mis ojos,
aliviará la angustia de otro corazón
devorado por las nebulosas.

No nos salva la gente de las zapaterías,
ni los paisajes que se hacen música al encontrar las llaves
    oxidadas.
Son mentira los aires. Solo existe
una cunita en el desván
que recuerda todas las cosas.
Y la luna.
Pero no la luna.
Los insectos,
los insectos solos,
crepitantes, mordientes, estremecidos, agrupados,
y la luna
con un guante de humo sentada en la puerta de sus derribos.
¡¡La luna!!

New York, 4 de enero de 1930

And in Peru one thousand women live, O insects, who night
    and day
make nocturnes and parades braiding their own veins.

A tiny corrosive glove detains me. Enough!
In my handkerchief I have felt the crack
of the first vein breaking.
Take care with your feet, my love, your hands,
since I have to give away my face,
oh, my face, my eaten face!

These chaste flames for my desire,
this confusion longing for balance,
this innocent sorrow of gunpowder in my eyes,
will ease the anguish of another heart
devoured by nebulae.

The people in the shoe stores do not save us,
or the landscapes that become music when they find the rusted
    keys.
The airs are lies. Only a small cradle
in the attic exists
and it remembers everything.
And the moon.
But not the moon.
The insects,
the insects alone,
cracking, biting, shaken, swarming,
and the moon
with a glove of smoke seated at the door of its ruins.
The moon!

New York, January 4, 1930

Federico García Lorca / 119

VII
Vuelta a la ciudad

Para Antonio Hernández Soriano

VII
Return to the City

For Antonio Hernández Soriano

NEW YORK
Oficina y Denuncia
                    A Fernando Vela

Debajo de las multiplicaciones
hay una gota de sangre de pato.
Debajo de las divisiones
hay una gota de sangre de marinero.
Debajo de las sumas, un río de sangre tierna;
un río que viene cantando
por los dormitorios de los arrabales,
y es plata, cemento o brisa
en el alba mentida de New York.
Existen las montañas, lo sé.
Y los anteojos para la sabiduría,
lo sé. Pero yo no he venido a ver el cielo.
He venido para ver la turbia sangre,
la sangre que lleva las máquinas a las cataratas
y el espíritu a la lengua de la cobra.
Todos los días se matan en New York
cuatro millones de patos,
cinco millones de cerdos,
dos mil palomas para el gusto de los agonizantes,
un millón de vacas,
un millón de corderos
y dos millones de gallos,
que dejan los cielos hechos añicos.
Más vale sollozar afilando la navaja
o asesinar a los perros en las alucinantes cacerías,
que resistir en la madrugada
los interminables trenes de leche,
los interminables trenes de sangre
y los trenes de rosas maniatadas
por los comerciantes de perfumes.

NEW YORK
Office and Denunciation
To Fernando Vela

Under the multiplications
there is a drop of duck's blood.
Under the divisions
there is a drop of sailor's blood.
Under the sums, a river of tender blood;
a river that sings its way
through outlying bedrooms,
and it is silver, cement or breeze
in the false dawn of New York.
The mountains exist, I know it.
And eyeglasses for wisdom,
I know. But I haven't come to see the sky.
I have come to see the muddled blood
that sends machines to the waterfall
and the spirit to the cobra's tongue.
Every day in New York they slaughter
four million ducks,
five million pigs,
two thousand doves for the pleasure of the dying,
a million cows,
a million lambs,
and two million roosters
that leave the sky in splinters.
Better to weep sharpening the blade
or murder the dogs in the hallucinating hunts
than resist at dawn
the endless trains of milk,
the endless trains of blood,
the trains packed with roses handcuffed
by the perfume merchants.

Los patos y las palomas,
y los cerdos y los corderos
ponen sus gotas de sangre
debajo de las multiplicaciones,
y los terribles alaridos de las vacas estrujadas
llenan de dolor el valle
donde el Hudson se emborracha con aceite.
Yo denuncio a toda la gente
que ignora la otra mitad,
la mitad irredimible
que levanta sus montes de cemento
donde laten los corazones
de los animalitos que se olvidan
y donde caeremos todos
en la última fiesta de los taladros.
Os escupo en la cara.
La otra mitad me escucha
devorando, cantando, volando en su pureza,
como los niños de las porterías
que llevan frágiles palitos
a los huecos donde se oxidan
las antenas de los insectos.
No es el infierno, es la calle.
No es la muerte, es la tienda de frutas.
Hay un mundo de ríos quebrados y distancias inasibles
en la patita de ese gato quebrada por el automóvil,
y yo oigo el canto de la lombriz
en el corazón de muchas niñas.
Óxido, fermento, tierra estremecida.
Tierra tú mismo que nadas por los números de la oficina.
¿Qué voy a hacer, ordenar los paisajes?

The ducks and the doves
and the pigs and the lambs
lay their drops of blood
under the multiplications;
and the terrible cries of crushed cows
fill the valley with sorrow
where the Hudson gets drunk on oil.
I denounce all of the people
who ignore the other half,
the unredeemable half,
who raise their mountains of cement
over the still-beating hearts
of small forsaken animals
and where we are headed
in the final feast of jackhammers.
I spit on your faces.
The other half listens to me,
devouring, urinating, flying in its innocence,
like the boys in the doorways
who place fragile sticks
into holes where the antennae
of insects rust.
This isn't hell, it's the street.
This isn't death, it's the fruit store.
There is a world of broken rivers
and infinite distances
in the cat's leg crushed by a car,
and I hear the worm's song
in the heart of many girls.
Rust, ferment, shaken earth.
Earth yourself swimming
through the numbers in the offices.
What can I do, bring order to the landscape?

¿Ordenar los amores que luego son fotografías,
que luego son pedazos de madera y bocanadas de sangre?
No, no; yo denuncio.
Yo denuncio la conjura
de estas desiertas oficinas
que no radian las agonías,
que borran los programas de la selva,
y me ofrezco a ser comido por las vacas estrujadas
cuando sus gritos llenan el valle
donde el Hudson se emborracha con aceite.

Bring order to the many loves
who will, in time, turn to photographs
and then pieces of wood and mouthfuls of blood?
No, no. I denounce.
I denounce the conspiracy
of those deserted offices
swept clean of agony
that erase the designs of the forest,
and I offer myself to be eaten by the crushed cows
when their screams fill the valley
where the Hudson gets drunk on oil.

CEMENTERIO JUDÍO

Las alegres fiebres huyeron a las maromas de los barcos
y el judío empujó la verja con el pudor helado del interior
de la lechuga.

Los niños de Cristo dormían,
y el agua era una paloma,
y la madera era una garza,
y el plomo era un colibrí,
y aun las vivas prisiones de fuego
estaban consoladas por el salto de la langosta.

Los niños de Cristo bogaban y los judíos llenaban los muros
con un solo corazón de paloma
por el que todos querían escapar.
Las niñas de Cristo cantaban y las judías miraban la muerte
con un solo ojo de faisán,
vidriado por la angustia de un millón de paisajes.

Los médicos ponen en el níquel sus tijeras y guantes de goma
cuando los cadáveres sienten en los pies
la terrible claridad de otra luna enterrada.
Pequeños dolores ilesos se acercan a los hospitales
y los muertos se van quitando un traje de sangre cada día.

Las arquitecturas de escarcha,
las liras y gemidos que se escapan de las hojas diminutas
en otoño, mojando las últimas vertientes,
se apagaban en el negro de los sombreros de copa.

La hierba celeste y sola de la que huye con miedo el rocío
y las blancas entradas de mármol que conducen al aire duro
mostraban su silencio roto por las huellas dormidas de los
        zapatos.

JEWISH CEMETERY

The happy fevers fled to the cable of the boats
and with the icy shyness inside the lettuce
the Jew pushed the gate.

The children of Christ were sleeping
and the water was a dove,
the wood a heron,
the lead a hummingbird,
and even the living prisons of fire
were consoled by the lobster's leap.

The boys of Christ rowed and the Jews filled the walls
with a single heart of dove
through which all wanted to escape.
The girls of Christ sang and the Jewish women looked at death
with a single eye of pheasant,
glazed by the anguish of a million landscapes.

The doctors place into nickel their scissors and rubber gloves
when the cadavers feel in their feet
the terrible clarity of another buried moon.
Small unhurt sorrows approach the hospitals
and every day the dead take off a suit of blood.

The architectures of frost,
the lyres and moans that escape the tiny leaves
in autumn, soaking the final slopes,
died out in the blackness of felt hats.

The lone heavenly herb the dew flees in fear,
and the white entries of marble leading to the hard air
showed their silence broken by the sleeping prints of shoes.

Federico García Lorca / 129

El judío empujó la verja;
pero el judío no era un puerto,
y las barcas de nieve se agolparon
por las escalerillas de su corazón:
las barcas de nieve que acechan
un hombre de agua que las ahogue,
las barcas de los cementerios
que a veces dejan ciegos a los visitantes.

Los niños de Cristo dormían
y el judío ocupó su litera.
Tres mil judíos lloraban en el espanto de las galerías
porque reunían entre todos con esfuerzo media paloma,
porque uno tenía la rueda de un reloj
y otro un botín con orugas parlantes
y otro una lluvia nocturna cargada de cadenas
y otro la uña de un ruiseñor que estaba vivo;
y porque la media paloma gemía
derramando una sangre que no era la suya.

Las alegres fiebres bailaban por las cúpulas humedecidas
y la luna copiaba en su mármol
nombres viejos y cintas ajadas.
Llegó la gente que come por detrás de las yertas columnas
y los asnos de blancos dientes
con los especialistas de las articulaciones.
Verdes girasoles temblaban
por los páramos del crepúsculo
y todo el cementerio era una queja
de bocas de cartón y trapo seco.
Ya los niños de Cristo se dormían
cuando el judío, apretando los ojos,
se cortó las manos en silencio
al escuchar los primeros gemidos.

New York, 18 de enero de 1930

The Jew pushed the gate;
but the Jew was not a port
and the boats of snow struck
the gangways of his heart:
the boats of snow that stalk
a man of water who might drown them,
the boats of cemeteries
that sometimes leave the visitors blind.

The children of Christ slept
and the Jew was in his bunk.
Despite all their efforts, three thousand Jews had half a dove
because one had the wheel of a clock
and another a boot with talking caterpillars
and another a nocturnal rain weighted by chains
and another a still living nightingale's claw;
and because the half dove moaned,
spilling blood not its own,
in dread of the galleries, the three thousand Jews wept.

The happy fevers danced on the humid domes
and the moon inscribed in its marble
old names and crumpled ribbons.
Then came the people who eat behind the ruined columns
carrying the asses of white teeth
with the doctors of articulations.
Green sunflowers trembled
in the wilderness of dusk
and the whole cemetery was a complaint
of cardboard mouths and dry rags.
While the children of Christ were already sleeping,
the Jew, squeezing shut his eyes,
cut his hands in silence
when he heard the first moans.

New York, January 18, 1930

PEQUEÑO POEMA INFINITO

Para Luis Cardoza y Aragón

Equivocar el camino
es llegar a la nieve
y llegar a la nieve
es pacer durante varios siglos las hierbas de los cementerios.

Equivocar el camino
es llegar a la mujer,
la mujer que no teme la luz,
la mujer que mata dos gallos en un segundo,
la luz que no teme a los gallos
y los gallos que no saben cantar sobre la nieve.

Pero si la nieve se equivoca de corazón
puede llegar el viento Austro
y como el aire no hace caso de los gemidos
tendremos que pacer otra vez las hierbas de los cementerios.

Yo vi dos dolorosas espigas de cera
que enterraban un paisaje de volcanes
y vi dos niños locos que empujaban llorando las pupilas de un
    asesino.

Pero el dos no ha sido nunca un número
porque es una angustia y su sombra,
porque es la guitarra donde el amor se desespera,
porque es la demostración de otro infinito que no es suyo
y es las murallas del muerto
y el castigo de la nueva resurrección sin finales.

SMALL INFINITE POEM

For Luis Cardoza y Aragón

To mistake the road
is to arrive at snow
and to arrive at snow
is to graze for twenty centuries on cemetery grasses.

To mistake the road
is to arrive at woman,
woman unafraid of light,
woman who murders two roosters in a second,
light unafraid of roosters
and roosters that don't know how to sing over snow.

But if the snow mistakes the heart
the south wind can come
and as the air takes no notice of the moan
we will have to graze again on cemetery grasses.

I saw two pained stalks of wax
that buried a landscape of volcanoes
and I saw two crazy crying boys who pushed a murderer's
    pupils.

But two has never been a number
because it is anguish and it is shadow,
because it is a guitar where love despairs,
because it is the proof of another infinity that isn't its own
and it is the walls of the dead man
and the punishment of a new, unending resurrection.

Federico García Lorca / 133

Los muertos odian el número dos,
pero el número dos adormece a las mujeres
y como la mujer teme la luz
la luz tiembla delante de los gallos
y los gallos solo saben volar sobre la nieve
tendremos que pacer sin descanso las hierbas de los cementerios.

New York, 10 de enero de 1930

The dead hate the number two
but the number two puts women to sleep
and as woman fears light
light trembles before the roosters
and as roosters alone know how to fly over snow
we will have to graze without rest on cemetery grasses.

New York, January 10, 1930

CRUCIFIXIÓN

La luna pudo detenerse al fin por la curva blanquísima de los
   caballos.
Un rayo de luz violenta que se escapaba de la herida
proyectó en el cielo el instante de la circuncisión de un niño
   muerto.

La sangre bajaba por el monte y los ángeles la buscaban,
pero los cálices eran de viento y al fin llenaba los zapatos.
Cojos perros fumaban sus pipas y un olor de cuero caliente
ponía grises los labios redondos de los que vomitaban en las
   esquinas.
Y llegaban largos alaridos por el Sur de la noche seca.
Era que la luna quemaba con sus bujías el falo de los caballos.
Un sastre especialista en púrpura
había encerrado a tres santas mujeres
y les enseñaba una calavera por los vidrios de la ventana.
Las tres en el arrabal rodeaban a un camello blanco
que lloraba porque al alba
tenía que pasar sin remedio por el ojo de una aguja.
¡Oh cruz! ¡Oh clavos! ¡Oh espina!
¡Oh espina clavada en el hueso hasta que se oxiden los
   planetas!
Como nadie volvía la cabeza, el cielo pudo desnudarse.
Entonces se oyó la gran voz y los fariseos dijeron:
Esa maldita vaca tiene las tetas llenas de leche.
La muchedumbre cerraba las puertas
y la lluvia bajaba por las calles decidida a mojar el corazón
mientras la tarde se puso turbia de latidos y leñadores
y la oscura ciudad agonizaba bajo el martillo de los carpinteros.

CRUCIFIXION

The moon could stop at last on the whitest curve of the horses.
A ray of violent light escaped from the wound
and projected on the sky the instant of a dead boy's
     circumcision.

Blood flowed down the mountain and the angels looked for it,
but the chalices were wind and the blood finally filled the
     shoes.
Lame dogs smoked their pipes and a smell of hot leather
made gray the round lips of those who vomited on street
     corners.
And from the South of the dry night long howls arrived.
It was the moon with its candle burning the phalluses of horses.
A tailor, specialist in purple,
had shut away three saintly women
and showed them a skull through the window glass.
In the outskirts all three surrounded a white camel
that wept because at dawn
it had to pass through the eye of a needle.
O cross! O nails! O thorn!
O thorn nailed to bone until the planets rust!
Since no one turned to look, the sky stripped naked.
Then we heard the great voice and the Pharisees said:
That damned cow has teats full of milk.
The rabble shut the doors
and the rain came down the street determined to soak the heart
while the afternoon grew troubled with heartbeats and
     woodsmen
and the dark city agonized under the hammer of carpenters.

Federico García Lorca / 137

Esa maldita vaca
tiene las tetas llenas de perdigones,
dijeron los fariseos.
Pero la sangre mojó sus pies y los espíritus inmundos
estrellaban ampollas de laguna sobre las paredes del templo.
Se supo el momento preciso de la salvación de nuestra vida.
Porque la luna lavó con agua
las quemaduras de los caballos
y no la niña viva que callaron en la arena.
Entonces salieron los fríos cantando sus canciones
y las ranas encendieron sus lumbres en la doble orilla del río.
Esa maldita vaca, maldita, maldita, maldita
no nos dejará dormir, dijeron los fariseos,
y se alejaron a sus casas por el tumulto de la calle
dando empujones a los borrachos y escupiendo sal de los
      sacrificios
mientras la sangre los seguía con un balido de cordero.

Fue entonces
y la tierra despertó arrojando temblorosos ríos de polilla.

New York, 18 de octubre de 1929

That damned cow
has teats full of buckshot,
the Pharisees said.
But blood wet their feet and the lowly spirits
burst lake blisters on the walls of the temple.
We learned the precise moment of our lives' salvation.
Because the moon washed with water
the burns of the horses
and not the lively girl they silenced on the sand.
Then the cold came singing its songs
and the frogs lit their fires on the double shore of the river.
That damned, damned cow
won't let us sleep, said the Pharisees,
and they left for home through the tumult on the street,
pushing aside drunks and spitting the salt of
        sacrifice
while the blood pursued them bleating like a lamb.

That was then
and the earth awoke hurling tremulous rivers of moths.

New York, October 18, 1929

VIII
Dos odas

A mi editor, Armando Guibert

VIII
Two Odes

To my editor, Armando Guibert

GRITO HACIA ROMA
(desde la torre del Chrysler Building)

Manzanas levemente heridas
por finos espadines de plata,
nubes rasgadas por una mano de coral
que lleva en el dorso una almendra de fuego,
peces de arsénico como tiburones,
tiburones como gotas de llanto para cegar una multitud,
rosas que hieren
y agujas instaladas en los caños de la sangre,
mundos enemigos y amores cubiertos de gusanos
caerán sobre ti. Caerán sobre la gran cúpula
que untan de aceite las lenguas militares
donde un hombre se orina en una deslumbrante paloma
y escupe carbón machacado
rodeado de miles de campanillas.

Porque ya no hay quien reparta el pan ni el vino,
ni quien cultive hierbas en la boca del muerto,
ni quien abra los linos del reposo,
ni quien llore por las heridas de los elefantes.
No hay más que un millón de herreros
forjando cadenas para los niños que han de venir.
No hay más que un millón de carpinteros
que hacen ataúdes sin cruz.
No hay más que un gentío de lamentos
que se abren las ropas en espera de la bala.
El hombre que desprecia la paloma debía hablar,
debía gritar desnudo entre las columnas,
y ponerse una inyección para adquirir la lepra
y llorar un llanto tan terrible
que disolviera sus anillos y sus teléfonos de diamante.
Pero el hombre vestido de blanco
ignora el misterio de la espiga,

CRY TOWARD ROME
(From the Tower of the Chrysler Building)

Apples slightly wounded
by fine short swords of silver,
clouds scraped by a hand of coral
with an almond of fire on its back,
arsenic fish like sharks,
sharks like teardrops that blind the crowds,
roses that wound
and needles installed in the pipes of blood,
enemy worlds and loves covered by worms
will fall on you. They will fall on the great dome
the military tongues coat with oil,
where a man urinates on a dazzling dove
and spits out ground coal
surrounded by thousands of handbells.

Because there is no one now to offer bread or wine
or tend to the grass in the dead man's mouth,
no one to open the linens of repose
or weep for wounded elephants.
There are only a million iron workers
forging chains for the children to come.
There are only a million carpenters
who make coffins without crosses.
There is only a crowd of laments
that undo their clothes and wait for a bullet.
The man who despises the dove should speak,
should scream naked among the columns,
and inject himself with leprosy
and cry a lament so horrible it might dissolve
his rings and his diamond telephones.
But the man in white
ignores the mystery of the wheat stalk,

ignora el gemido de la parturienta,
ignora que Cristo puede dar agua todavía,
ignora que la moneda quema el beso de prodigio
y da la sangre del cordero al pico idiota del faisán.

Los maestros enseñan a los niños
una luz maravillosa que viene del monte;
pero lo que llega es una reunión de cloacas
donde gritan las oscuras ninfas del cólera.
Los maestros señalan con devoción las enormes cúpulas
        sahumadas;
pero debajo de las estatuas no hay amor,
no hay amor bajo los ojos de cristal definitivo.
El amor está en las carnes desgarradas por la sed,
en la choza diminuta que lucha con la inundación;
el amor está en los fosos donde luchan las sierpes del hambre,
en el triste mar que mece los cadáveres de las gaviotas
y en el oscurísimo beso punzante debajo de las almohadas.
Pero el viejo de las manos traslúcidas
dirá: amor, amor, amor,
aclamado por millones de moribundos;
dirá: amor, amor, amor,
entre el tisú estremecido de ternura;
dirá: paz, paz, paz,
entre el tirite de cuchillos y melones de dinamita;
dirá: amor, amor, amor,
hasta que se le pongan de plata los labios.

Mientras tanto, mientras tanto, ¡ay!, mientras tanto,
los negros que sacan las escupideras,
los muchachos que tiemblan bajo el terror pálido de los
        directores,
las mujeres ahogadas en aceites minerales,
la muchedumbre de martillo, de violín o de nube,
ha de gritar aunque le estrellen los sesos en el muro,

ignores the moan of the woman in labor,
ignores that Christ can still give water,
ignores that the coin burns the prodigal kiss,
and he gives the lamb's blood to the idiot beak of the pheasant.

Teachers teach children
of a marvelous light that comes from the mount
but what comes is a gathering of sewers
where the dark nymphs of cholera scream.
The teachers point with devotion to the huge censered
    domes,
but beneath the statues there is no love,
no love inside the eyes of ultimate crystal.
Love is in the flesh torn apart by thirst,
love is in the small shack that struggles with floods;
love is in the pits where the snakes of hunger struggle,
in the sad sea that rocks the bodies of dead seagulls,
and in the darkest piercing kiss under the pillows.
But the old man with translucent hands
will say: love, love,
acclaimed by moribund millions;
will say: love, love
into the tissue shaken by tenderness;
will say: peace, peace
between the shivering knives and the dynamite melons;
will say: love, love
until his lips turn to silver.

Meanwhile, meanwhile, meanwhile,
the blacks who empty the spittoons,
the boys who tremble before the pale terror of
    managers,
the women drowned in mineral oils,
the masses of hammer, violin, or cloud,
must cry although their brains are smashed against the wall,

ha de gritar frente a las cúpulas,
ha de gritar loca de fuego,
ha de gritar loca de nieve,
ha de gritar con la cabeza llena de excremento,
ha de gritar como todas las noches juntas,
ha de gritar con voz tan desgarrada
hasta que las ciudades tiemblen como niñas
y rompan las prisiones del aceite y la música,
porque queremos el pan nuestro de cada día,
flor de aliso y perenne ternura desgranada,
porque queremos que se cumpla la voluntad de la Tierra
que da sus frutos para todos.

must cry before the domes,
must cry maddened by fire,
must cry maddened by snow,
must cry with their head full of excrement,
must cry like all the nights together,
must cry in a voice so broken
the cities will tremble like girls
and break the prisons of oil and music,
because we want our daily bread,
alder flowers and perennial threshed tenderness,
because we want the Earth's will be done
to give its fruits to all.

ODA A WALT WHITMAN

Por el East River y el Bronx
los muchachos cantaban enseñando sus cinturas,
con la rueda, el aceite, el cuero y el martillo.
Noventa mil mineros sacaban la plata de las rocas
y los niños dibujaban escaleras y perspectivas.

Pero ninguno se dormía,
ninguno quería ser el río,
ninguno amaba las hojas grandes,
ninguno la lengua azul de la playa.

Por el East River y el Queensborough
los muchachos luchaban con la industria,
y los judíos vendían al fauno del río
la rosa de la circuncisión
y el cielo desembocaba por los puentes y los tejados
manadas de bisontes empujadas por el viento.

Pero ninguno se detenía,
ninguno quería ser nube,
ninguno buscaba los helechos
ni la rueda amarilla del tamboril.

Cuando la luna salga
las poleas rodarán para turbar el cielo;
un límite de agujas cercará la memoria
y los ataúdes se llevarán a los que no trabajan.

Nueva York de cieno,
Nueva York de alambre y de muerte.
¿Qué ángel llevas oculto en la mejilla?
¿Qué voz perfecta dirá las verdades del trigo?
¿Quién el sueño terrible de tus anémonas manchadas?

ODE TO WALT WHITMAN

By the East River and the Bronx
the young men sang, baring their waists
with the wheel, the oil, the hide, and the hammer.
Ninety thousand miners mined silver from the rocks
and the children drew stairwells and perspectives.

But none fell asleep,
none wished to be the river,
none loved the large leaves
or the beach's blue tongue.

By the East River and the Queensboro
the young men wrestled with industry
and the Jews sold the rose of circumcision
to the faun of the river
and the sky spilled over bridges and rooftops
herds of buffalo pushed by the wind.

But none stopped,
none wished to be a cloud,
none looked for ferns
or the yellow wheel of the drum.

When the moon rises
the pulleys will turn to trouble the sky;
a border of needles will circle memory
and coffins will carry off those who don't work.

New York of filth,
New York of wires and death.
What angel do you carry hidden in your cheek?
What perfect voice will speak the truths of wheat?
Who the terrible dreams of your stained anemones?

Federico García Lorca / 149

Ni un solo momento, viejo hermoso Walt Whitman,
he dejado de ver tu barba llena de mariposas,
ni tus hombros de pana gastados por la luna,
ni tus muslos de Apolo virginal,
ni tu voz como una columna de ceniza;
anciano hermoso como la niebla
que gemías igual que un pájaro
con el sexo atravesado por una aguja,
enemigo del sátiro,
enemigo de la vid
y amante de los cuerpos bajo la burda tela.
Ni un solo momento, hermosura viril
que en montes de carbón, anuncios y ferrocarriles,
soñabas ser un río y dormir como un río
con aquel camarada que pondría en tu pecho
un pequeño dolor de ignorante leopardo.

Ni un solo momento, Adán de sangre, macho,
hombre solo en el mar, viejo hermoso Walt Whitman,
porque por las azoteas,
agrupados en los bares,
saliendo en racimos de las alcantarillas,
temblando entre las piernas de los chauffeurs
o girando en las plataformas del ajenjo,
los maricas, Walt Whitman, te señalan.

¡También ese! ¡También! Y se despeñan
sobre tu barba luminosa y casta,
rubios del norte, negros de la arena,
muchedumbres de gritos y ademanes,
como gatos y como las serpientes,
los maricas, Walt Whitman, los maricas
turbios de lágrimas, carne para fusta,
bota o mordisco de los domadores.

Not for one moment, beautiful old Walt Whitman,
have I not seen your beard full of butterflies,
or your corduroy shoulders worn away by the moon,
or your virginal Apollo thighs,
or your voice like a column of ash;
beautiful old man like the mist,
who cried like a bird
with its sex pierced by a needle.
Enemy of the satyr,
enemy of the vine
and lover of bodies under coarse cloth.
Not for one moment, virile beauty
on mountains of coal, billboards, and railroads,
did you dream of being a river and sleeping like a river
with that comrade who would place in your chest
the small sorrow of an ignorant leopard.

Not for a single moment, macho Adam of blood,
man alone at sea, beautiful old Walt Whitman,
because on rooftops,
gathered in bars,
leaving the sewers in bunches,
trembling between the legs of chauffeurs,
or spinning on platforms of absinthe,
the queers, Walt Whitman, are pointing at you.

That one, too! That one! And they hurl themselves
on your chaste and luminous beard,
blonds from the north, blacks from the sands,
crowds of cries and gestures
like cats and like snakes,
the queers, Walt Whitman, the queers,
their troubled tears, meat for the whip,
the boot or bite of their masters.

¡También ese! ¡También! Dedos teñidos
apuntan a la orilla de tu sueño
cuando el amigo come tu manzana
con un leve sabor de gasolina
y el sol canta por los ombligos
de los muchachos que juegan bajo los puentes.

Pero tú no buscabas los ojos arañados,
ni el pantano oscurísimo donde sumergen a los niños,
ni la saliva helada,
ni las curvas heridas como panza de sapo
que llevan los maricas en coches y terrazas
mientras la luna los azota por las esquinas del terror.

Tú buscabas un desnudo que fuera como un río,
toro y sueño que junte la rueda con el alga,
padre de tu agonía, camelia de tu muerte,
y gimiera en las llamas de tu ecuador oculto.

Porque es justo que el hombre no busque su deleite
en la selva de sangre de la mañana próxima.
El cielo tiene playas donde evitar la vida
y hay cuerpos que no deben repetirse en la aurora.

Agonía, agonía, sueño, fermento y sueño.
Este es el mundo, amigo, agonía, agonía.
Los muertos se descomponen bajo el reloj de las ciudades,
la guerra pasa llorando con un millón de ratas grises,
los ricos dan a sus queridas
pequeños moribundos iluminados,
y la vida no es noble, ni buena, ni sagrada.

Puede el hombre, si quiere, conducir su deseo
por vena de coral o celeste desnudo.
Mañana los amores serán rocas y el Tiempo
una brisa que viene dormida por las ramas.

That one too! That one! Stained fingers
point at the shore of your dream,
when a friend eats your apple
with a slight taste of gasoline
and the sun sings in the navels
of the young men playing under the bridge.

But you weren't looking for scratched eyes,
or the darkest swamp where they submerge the boys,
or the frozen saliva,
or the curved wounds like the belly of a toad
the queers wear in cars and on terraces
while the moon whips them through the corners of terror.

You looked for a nude that might be a river
and moan in the flames of your hidden equator,
bull and dream that join the wheel with seaweed,
father of your agony, camellia of your death.

Because it's fitting that a man not seek his pleasure
in the bloody jungles of tomorrow morning.
The sky has beaches where life is avoided
and there are bodies that shouldn't repeat themselves at dawn.

Agony, agony, dream, ferment, and dream.
This is the world, friend, agony.
The dead decompose below the clocks of the cities,
war passes weeping with a million gray rats,
the rich give their lovers
small illuminated deaths,
and life is not noble, or good, or sacred.

If he wishes, man can guide his desires
through a vein of coral or naked blue sky.
Tomorrow the lovers will be stone and Time
a breeze that walks sleeping through the branches.

Federico García Lorca / 153

Por eso no levanto mi voz, viejo Walt Whitman,
contra el niño que escribe
nombre de niña en su almohada,
ni contra el muchacho que se viste de novia
en la oscuridad del ropero,
ni contra los solitarios de los casinos
que beben con asco el agua de la prostitución,
ni contra los hombres de mirada verde
que aman al hombre y queman sus labios en silencio.
Pero sí contra vosotros, maricas de las ciudades,
de carne tumefacta y pensamiento inmundo,
madres de lodo, arpías, enemigos sin sueño
del Amor que reparte coronas de alegría.

Contra vosotros siempre, que dais a los muchachos
gotas de sucia muerte con amargo veneno.
Contra vosotros siempre,
Faeries de Norteamérica,
Pájaros de la Habana,
Jotos de Méjico,
Sarasas de Cádiz,
Apios de Sevilla,
Cancos de Madrid,
Floras de Alicante,
Adelaidas de Portugal.

¡Maricas de todo el mundo, asesinos de palomas!
Esclavos de la mujer, perras de sus tocadores,
abiertos en las plazas con fiebre de abanico
o emboscados en yertos paisajes de cicuta.

¡No haya cuartel! La muerte
mana de vuestros ojos
y agrupa flores grises en la orilla del cieno.
¡No haya cuartel! ¡Alerta!

And so, I don't raise my voice, old Walt Whitman,
against the boy who writes
a girl's name on his pillow,
or against the young man who dresses like a bride
in the darkness of his closet,
or the solitary men in the casinos
who drink with disgust the water of prostitution,
or the green men who leer, who love
other men and burn their lips in silence.
But I will against you, queers of the cities,
of tumescent flesh and filthy thought,
mothers of mud, harpies, dreamless enemies
of the Love that delivers crowns of joy.

Against you always, who give young men
drops of dirty death with bitter poison.
Against you always,
Fairies of North America,
Pájaros of Havana,
Jotos of Mexico,
Sarasas of Cádiz,
Apios of Seville,
Cancos of Madrid,
Floras of Alicante,
Adelaidas of Portugal.

Queers of the world, assassins of doves!
Slaves of women, bitches of their dressing rooms,
open in the plazas with a fan-like fever
or ambushed in stiff landscapes of hemlock.

No mercy! Death
pours out of your eyes
and clusters gray flowers on the shores of filth.
No mercy! Look!

Que los confundidos, los puros,
los clásicos, los señalados, los suplicantes
os cierren las puertas de la bacanal.

Y tú, bello Walt Whitman, duerme a orillas del
      Hudson
con la barba hacia el polo y las manos abiertas.
Arcilla blanda o nieve, tu lengua está llamando
camaradas que velen tu gacela sin cuerpo.
Duerme, no queda nada.
Una danza de muros agita las praderas
y América se anega de máquinas y llanto.
Quiero que el aire fuerte de la noche más honda
quite flores y letras del arco donde duermes
y un niño negro anuncie a los blancos del oro
la llegada del reino de la espiga.

Let the confused, the pure,
the classical, the chosen, the supplicants
shut on you the doors of the bacchanal.

And you, beautiful Walt Whitman, sleep on the shores of the
     Hudson
with your beard pointed toward the pole and your hands open.
Soft clay or snow, your tongue is calling
comrades to watch over your bodiless gazelle.
Sleep: nothing remains.
A dance of walls shakes the prairies
and America sinks into machines and tears.
I want the strong airs of deepest night
to remove the flowers and letters from the arch where you sleep
and a black boy to announce to the white golden ones
the arrival of the kingdom of grain.

IX
Huida de Nueva York

Dos valses hacia la civilización

IX
Flight from New York

Two Waltzes Toward Civilization

PEQUEÑO VALS VIENÉS

En Viena hay diez muchachas,
un hombro donde solloza la muerte
y un bosque de palomas disecadas.
Hay un fragmento de la mañana
en el museo de la escarcha.
Hay un salón con mil ventanas.
    ¡Ay, ay, ay, ay!
Toma este vals con la boca cerrada.

Este vals, este vals, este vals,
de sí, de muerte y de coñac
que moja su cola en el mar.

Te quiero, te quiero, te quiero,
con la butaca y el libro muerto,
por el melancólico pasillo,
en el oscuro desván del lirio,
en nuestra cama de la luna
y en la danza que sueña la tortuga.
    ¡Ay, ay, ay, ay!
Toma este vals de quebrada cintura.

En Viena hay cuatro espejos
donde juegan tu boca y los ecos.
Hay una muerte para piano
que pinta de azul a los muchachos.
Hay mendigos por los tejados.
Hay frescas guirnaldas de llanto.
    ¡Ay, ay, ay, ay!
Toma este vals que se muere en mis brazos.

SMALL VIENNESE WALTZ

In Vienna there are ten girls,
a shoulder on which death is sobbing
and a forest of dried-out pigeons.
There is a fragment of morning
in the museum of frost.
There is a salon with a thousand windows.
          Ay!
Take this waltz with your mouth closed.

This waltz, this waltz,
about itself, about death and cognac
that wets its tail in the sea.

I love you, I love you,
with the armchair and the dead book,
through the melancholy hallway,
in the dark attic of lilies,
on our bed of the moon
and the dance dreamed by the tortoise.
          Ay!
Take this waltz of the broken waist.

In Vienna there are four mirrors
where your mouth and the echoes play.
There is death for the piano
that paints the boys blue.
There are beggars on rooftops.
There are fresh garlands of weeping.
          Ay!
Take this waltz that dies in my arms.

Porque te quiero, te quiero, amor mío,
en el desván donde juegan los niños,
soñando viejas luces de Hungría
por los rumores de la tarde tibia,
viendo ovejas y lirios de nieve
por el silencio oscuro de tu frente.
              ¡Ay, ay, ay, ay!
Toma este vals del «Te quiero siempre».

En Viena bailaré contigo
con un disfraz que tenga
cabeza de río.
¡Mira qué orillas tengo de jacintos!
Dejaré mi boca entre tus piernas,
mi alma en fotografías y azucenas,
y en las ondas oscuras de tu andar
quiero, amor mío, amor mío, dejar,
violín y sepulcro, las cintas del vals.

Because I want you, my love,
in the attic where the children play,
dreaming the old lights of Hungary
through the rumors of the warm afternoon,
seeing lambs and lilies of snow,
in the dark silence of your forehead.
      Ay!
Take this waltz called "I love you always."

In Vienna I'll dance with you
wearing a disguise
with the head of a river.
Look at the hyacinth shores I wear!
I will leave my mouth between your legs,
my soul in photographs and white lilies.
In the dark waves of your journey
I want, my love, to leave
—violin and tomb—the ribbons of waltz.

VALS EN LAS RAMAS

Cayó una hoja
y dos
y tres.
Por la luna nadaba un pez.
El agua duerme una hora
y el mar blanco duerme cien.
La dama
estaba muerta en la rama.
La monja
cantaba dentro de la toronja.
La niña
iba por el pino a la piña.
Y el pino
buscaba la plumilla del trino.
Pero el ruiseñor
lloraba sus heridas alrededor.
Y yo también
porque cayó una hoja
y dos
y tres.
Y una cabeza de cristal
y un violín de papel
y la nieve podría con el mundo
una a una
dos a dos
y tres a tres.
¡Oh duro marfil de carnes invisibles!
¡Oh golfo sin hormigas del amanecer!

WALTZ IN THE BRANCHES

A leaf fell
and two
and three.
A fish was swimming through the moon.
The water sleeps an hour
and the white sea sleeps one hundred.
The woman
was dead on the branch.
The nun
sang inside a grapefruit.
The girl
went from pine to pinecone.
And the pine
sought the trill's tiny feather.
But all around the nightingale
wept its wounds.
And I did too
because a leaf fell
and two
and three.
And a crystal head
and a paper violin
and the snow could deal with the world
one by one
two by two
and three by three.
O hard ivory of invisible flesh!
O ant-less gulf of dawn!

Con el muu de las ramas,
con el ay de las damas,
con el croo de las ranas
y el gloo amarillo de la miel.
Llegará un torso de sombra
coronado de laurel.
Será el cielo para el viento
duro como una pared
y las ramas desgajadas
se irán bailando con él.
Una a una
alrededor de la luna,
dos a dos
alrededor del sol,
y tres a tres
para que los marfiles se duerman bien.

With the *muu* of the branches
with the *ay* of the ladies
and the *cro* of the frogs,
and the yellow *gloo* of honey.
A torso of shadow will come,
crowned with laurel.
For the wind the sky will be
hard as a wall
and the stripped branches
will dance away with it.
One by one
around the moon,
two by two
around the sun,
and three by three
so the ivories sleep.

X
El Poeta llega a la Habana

A don Fernando Ortiz

X
The Poet Arrives in Havana

To Don Fernando Ortiz

SON DE NEGROS EN CUBA

Cuando llegue la luna llena
iré a Santiago de Cuba.
Iré a Santiago.
En un coche de agua negra.
Iré a Santiago.
Cantarán los techos de palmera.
Iré a Santiago.
Cuando la palma quiere ser cigüeña.
Iré a Santiago.
Y cuando quiere ser medusa el plátano.
Iré a Santiago.
Con la rubia cabeza de Fonseca.
Iré a Santiago.
Y con la rosa de Romeo y Julieta.
Iré a Santiago.
Mar de papel y plata de monedas.
Iré a Santiago.
¡Oh Cuba, oh ritmo de semillas secas!
Iré a Santiago.
¡Oh cintura caliente y gota de madera!
Iré a Santiago.
¡Arpa de troncos vivos, caimán, flor de tabaco!
Iré a Santiago.
Siempre dije que yo iría a Santiago
en un coche de agua negra.
Iré a Santiago.
Brisa y alcohol en las ruedas.
Iré a Santiago.
Mi coral en la tiniebla.
Iré a Santiago.
El mar ahogado en la arena.

SON OF BLACKS IN CUBA

When the full moon comes
I'll go to Santiago de Cuba.
I'll go to Santiago.
In a coach of black water.
I'll go to Santiago.
The palm roofs will sing.
I'll go to Santiago.
When the palm tree wants to be a stork.
I'll go to Santiago.
And when the plantain wants to be medusa.
I'll go to Santiago.
With the blond head of Fonseca.
I'll go to Santiago.
And the rose of Romeo and Juliet.
I'll go to Santiago.
Sea of paper and coins of silver.
I'll go to Santiago.
O Cuba, O rhythm of dry seeds!
I'll go to Santiago.
O hot waist and drop of wood!
I'll go to Santiago.
Harp of living trunks, caiman, flower of tobacco!
I'll go to Santiago.
I always said I would go to Santiago
in a coach of black water.
I'll go to Santiago.
Breeze and alcohol on the wheels.
I'll go to Santiago.
My coral in the gloom.
I'll go to Santiago.
The sea drowned in sand.

Federico García Lorca / 171

Iré a Santiago.
Calor blanco, fruta muerta.
Iré a Santiago.
¡O bovino frescor de cañavera!
¡O Cuba! ¡O curva de suspiro y barro!
Iré a Santiago.

I'll go to Santiago.
White heat, dead fruit.
I'll go to Santiago.
O bovine freshness of sugar cane!
O Cuba! O curve of sighs and clay!
I'll go to Santiago.

Acknowledgments

As translators, we wish to thank *los herederos* of Federico García Lorca for their generosity. Elaine Markson, our agent, and Gary Johnson, her assistant, provided invaluable encouragement and expertise. Elisabeth Schmitz and Grove/Atlantic showed unwavering faith in the project from the very beginning. We are grateful for the support of of our colleagues at Eugene Lang College, The New School for Liberal Arts, and the University of Nevada, Las Vegas. Beth Vogel, Katherine Koch, Karen Koch, Pablo Medina, Sr., and Ron Padgett read parts of the manuscript and offered helpful and timely suggestions. Also helpful was Edward Hirsch, who wrote the Foreword. The Black Mountain Institute provided invaluable administrative support. The Virginia Center for the Creative Arts provided a residency for Mark Statman. We are also grateful to the members and staff of the Association of Writers and Writing Programs for their interest and their response to this project. The careful work of our editorial associates, Carolina Baffi and Lara Tucker, aided us greatly with the preparation of the manuscript.

Notes on the Poems

On repetition: Lorca's use of repetition has two sources. The first can be found in his fondness for and studious attention to old lyrical forms such as the medieval romances, or ballads, the Moorish *khassidas* and *ghazals*, and the flamenco music he heard as a child in Andalusia. The second source is rooted in his abilities as a dramatist and his penchant for highly stylized melodrama in which repetition has both structural and emotive functions. Lorca often reaches for such effects in *Poet in New York* by repeating certain words (*ay, amor*, etc.). On occasion, we have chosen to cut down on the repetition for the sake of compactness and directness, both qualities that are paramount in contemporary poetry. For example: in "King of Harlem" Lorca repeats "Negros. Negros. Negros." The repetition in Spanish calls the reader's attention to the people and to his own sense of how to name a people and community, but it can sound highly artificial and clunky in English, not unlike the sound made by a car with a flat tire. The single "Blacks" here is meant to avoid these problems by maximizing the naming and minimizing the rhetorical excess.

On *Ay* and *Ay de mi*. These are difficult to translate. *Ay* can be read as oh or woe and *Ay de mi* as woe is me. But the Spanish *Ay* is almost sublingual, a more heartfelt cry than the English oh and *Ay de mi* does not have the anachronistic or superficial theatricality of woe is me. We have left them in the Spanish to get the full sense of a situation's emotional urgency, anxiety, confusion, etc., and in deference to Lorca's masterful handling of melodrama in critical moments in the poems.

The Generation of 1927 usually refers to a group of poets who rose to prominence in the mid-late 1920s. It is so named after a symposium held in Granada celebrating the tricentennial of the death of Góngora (1627), a poet much admired by these young writers, Lorca among them, and to distinguish them from the Generation of '98, which included Unamuno, Machado, Ortega y Gasset, and other prominent writers. Occasionally the label is extended to a larger group of artists who were affiliated with the younger poets (Salvador Dalí, Luis Buñuel). Lorca often refers to or quotes directly the work of his contemporaries in his poems.

Notes on the poems: *Poet in New York*

Carlos Morla Lynch (1885–1968) Chilean diplomat
Bebe Morla, married to Carlos Morla
Luis Cernuda (1902–1963) Spanish poet, "Generation of 1927"

Back from a Walk
Árbol de muñones refers literally to a tree that has had all its branches sheared off so that that only the trunk can be seen. We decided to translate the phrase as "limbless tree" emphasizing the absence of branches rather than the presence of stumps, for sound and also because the word *muñón* has no direct English equivalent.

1910
Lorca often told people he was born in 1900 (and not 1898) to suggest that he was a poet of the twentieth century. The age often represents for Lorca the end of childhood and the beginning of adulthood (like Blake's movement from innocence to experience).

Your Infancy in Mentón
The translation challenge here is with the *sin ti que no te entiende*, literally "without you that doesn't understand you," which we have translated as "fails to understand you" for Lorca's meaning and the line's music.

II. The Blacks

In the music, dance, and the living conditions of the Harlem community, Lorca senses a liveliness he empathizes with. He identifies with the apparently marginalized, those who are secretly disguised but still powerful spiritually (the king, for example) and who are known to those who know the signs.

Ángel del Río (1901–1962), Spanish writer and critic. A friend of Lorca in New York, he was a popular professor of Spanish at Columbia University.

The King of Harlem
Manzana, more commonly understood as apple, also has the meaning of street or block, with a sense of community and neighborhood.

Abandoned Church
see *Jewish Cemetery*

III. Streets and Dreams

Rafael Rodríguez Rapún (1912–1937), secretary and lover of Lorca; he died fighting with the Republicans in the Spanish Civil War.

Vicente Aleixandre (1898–1984), Spanish poet, "Generation of 27," Nobel Prize for Literature 1977.

Landscape of the Vomiting Crowd
Lorca visited Coney Island in December 1929, not in summer. Therefore, the scene here is an imagined one.

Murder
A display of Lorca the playwright, creating a dramatic situation based on an overheard conversation.

Birth of Christ
Translation of form by transposing form: Lorca writes here in Spanish Alexandrines, that is, fourteen-syllable lines divided by a caesura, or pause, into two hemistichs, or seven-syllable segments. Such syllabic length is nearly unmanageable in English and so we have resorted to a ten-syllable line in the translation.

IV. Poems of Lake Eden Mills

Eduardo Ugarte (1901–1955) Spanish writer and film director.

Double Poem of Lake Eden
Garcilaso de la Vega (ca 1501–1536) Spanish poet and soldier. Highly influenced by Italian literature, especially the pastoral tradition, he is considered one of the first Spanish poets to bring the humanism of the Renaissance to Spanish letters.

V. In the Farmer's Cabin

Concha Méndez (1898–1986) Spanish poet and editor, married to Manuel Altolaguirre.

Manuel Altolaguirre (1905–1959) Spanish poet and editor, "Generation of 27," married to Concha Méndez.

The Boy Stanton
Here Lorca writes about the transition between youth and adolescence (the cancer) and emerging questions of sex, love, and identity (see note on *1910*).

Girl Drowned in the Well
There was no girl who drowned while Lorca was visiting Newburgh. He is incorporating a memory of a story told when he was a boy in Granada.

The translation questions in this poem were connected with the repeated clause *"Que no desemboca,"* which we have translated using the negative participle: "Not flowing." The idea here is to suggest the well as the antithesis of the Heraklitean river, with not-so-subtle suggestions of Jorge Manrique's "Coplas": *"Nuestras vidas son los ríos que van a dar a la mar."* (Our lives are the rivers that flow out to sea.)

VI. Introduction to Death

Rafael Sánchez Ventura (1897–1984), Spanish professor of art history.

Nocturne of the Hole
"Nocturno del hueco" has usually been translated as "Nocturne of the Void" or "Nocturne of Emptiness." By translating *hueco* as "hole" we are being literal and charging the English version with the sexuality Lorca intended in his original.

Landscape with Two Tombs and an Assyrian Dog
see *Jewish Cemetery*

Ruin
Regino Sainz de la Maza (1896–1981) Spanish musician.

We were struck by the simple and stark connection of this poem to 9/11. Here the poet begins to emerge as a kind of oracle, a role he will take on with greater intensity in the poems that follow.

Moon and Panorama of the Insects
José de Espronceda (1808–1842) Spanish Romantic poet.

VII. Return to the City

New York: Office and Denunciation
Fernando Vela (1888–1966) Spanish critic.

The poet's oracular voice grows. He offers himself as a sacrifice to be eaten by the crushed cows.

Jewish Cemetery
In *Abandoned Church*, Lorca writes from the point of view of a parent. In *Landscape with Two Tombs and an Assyrian Dog*, he writes from the point of view of a friend. In *Jewish Cemetery*, he writes from the point of view of a spiritual visionary. The progression is consistent with the book's movement from chronicle to prophecy.

Sombrero de copa is literally a top hat. Lorca is referring, though, not to formal wear but to the hats worn by Hassidic Jews.

Small Infinite Poem and *Crucifixion*
These two poems were lost and not found until 1950. Several of Lorca's letters to friends reveal that he intended them for inclusion in *Poet in New York*, though he did not specify their exact placement in the book. We have included them here because they fit with the growing role of the poet as spiritual visionary evidenced in this section.

VIII. Two Odes

These represent the dramatic high point of the poet's journey, the poet as one who will not just denounce, not just sacrifice himself, but will speak for those who can't speak for themselves. This is a far cry from the poet who doesn't recognize his face, who is murdered by the sky, who is nostalgic for the childhood and can't admit love. Here Lorca is pronouncing to the world and longing for "the arrival of the kingdom of grain." These two poems, the most ambitious of the book, announce a Lorca who will be much in evidence when he returns to Spain from New York.

IX. Flight from New York

The waltzes, simple and playful, move toward civilization, which the city doesn't represent. Rather, think childhood and nature dancing around each other.

X. The Poet Arrives in Havana

Fernando Ortiz (1881–1969) Cuban ethnologist and musicologist, the first to recognize and highlight the importance of African elements in Cuban culture.

Son *of Blacks in Cuba*

Lorca is using the term *son* broadly here to mean tune or song, rather than specifically to refer to the type of Cuban music called *son* (the precursor of salsa), popularized in the last decade by the Buena Vista Social Club phenomenon. The poem in structure and refrain more closely resembles rumba, another type of Cuban music, which had its origins among the blacks in the barrios of Santiago de Cuba.

Lorca almost certainly meant to evoke the very Cuban *cañaveral*, meaning sugarcane field instead of *cañavera*, meaning reed-grass.

Luis Cardoza y Aragón (1904–1992) One of the most important Guatemalan poets of his time, rivaled in stature only by the Nobelist Miguel Ángel Asturias.

Further Reading

Guillermo Díaz-Plaja. *Federico García Lorca* (Espasa-Calpe, Madrid, 1954).

Daniel Eisenberg. *"Poeta en Nueva York*; historia y problemas de un texto de Lorca" (Biblioteca Virtual, Miguel de Cervantes, 1975).

Federico García Lorca. *In Search of Duende*, edited by Christopher Maurer (New Directions, New York, 1955, 1998).

———. *Obras Completas*, edited by Arturo del Hoyo with notes by Arturo del Hoyo, Jorge Guillén, and Vicente Aleixandre. (Aguilar, Madrid, 1980).

———. *Libro de poemas, Poema del cante jondo, Romancero gitano, Poeta en Nueva York, Odas, Llanto por Ignacio Sánchez Mejías, Bodas de sangre, Yerma*, prólogo de Salvador Novo (Editorial Porrúa, Mexico, 1989).

———. *Poeta en Nueva York, Llanto por Ignacio Sánchez Mejías, Diván del Tamarit* (Espasa-Calpe, Madrid, 1972).

———. *Poet in New York*, translated by Ben Belitt, introduction by Ángel del Río (Grove, New York, 1955).

———. *Poet in New York*, translated by Greg Simon and Steven F. White, edited and with an introduction by Christopher Maurer (Farrar, Straus & Giroux, New York, 1998).

——— and Salvador Dalí. *Sebastian's Arrows: Letters and Mementos of Federico García Lorca and Salvador Dalí*, edited by Christopher Maurer (Swan Isle Press, Chicago, 2004).

Isabel García Lorca. *Recuerdos míos* (Tusquets Editores, Barcelona, 2002).

Ian Gibson. *Federico García Lorca: A Life* (Pantheon, New York, 1989).

———. *Lorca's Granada: A Practical Guide* (Faber & Faber, London, 1992).

Edward Hirsch. *The Demon and the Angel* (Harcourt, San Diego & New York, 2002).

Leslie Stainton. *Lorca: A Dream of Life* (Farrar, Straus & Giroux, New York, 1999).